Great
Starters

Great Starters

Robert Carrier

Hamlyn London · New York · Sydney · Toronto

Photographs in this series taken by Christian Délu, John Miller, Jack Nisberg, Iain Reid, Pipe-Rich
Design by Martin Atcherley for The Nassington Press Ltd.
Line drawings by Vana Haggerty

Some material in this book has already been published in
The Robert Carrier Cookbook
Published in 1965 by
Thomas Nelson and Sons Ltd.
© Copyright Robert Carrier 1965

Published by
The Hamlyn Publishing Group Limited
London · New York · Sydney · Toronto
Astronaut House, Feltham, Middlesex, England

© Copyright Robert Carrier 1978

ISBN 0 600 32010 3

Printed in Italy

Contents

Useful Facts and Figures

Notes on metrication

When making any of the recipes in this book, only follow one set of measures as they are not interchangeable.

In this book quantities are given in metric and Imperial measures. Exact conversion from Imperial to metric measures does not usually give very convenient working quantities and so the metric measures have been rounded off into units of 25 grams. The table below shows the recommended equivalents.

Ounces	Approx gram to nearest whole figure	Recommended conversion to nearest unit of 25
1	28	25
2	57	50
3	85	75
4	113	100
5	142	150
6	170	175
7	198	200
8	227	225
9	255	250
10	283	275
11	312	300
12	340	350
13	368	375
14	396	400
15	425	425
16 (1 lb)	454	450
17	482	475
18	510	500
19	539	550
20 ($1\frac{1}{4}$ lb)	567	575

Note: When converting quantities over 20 oz first add the appropriate figures in the centre column, then adjust to the nearest unit of 25. As a general guide, 1 kg (1000 g) equals 2.2 lb or about 2 lb 3 oz. This method of conversion gives good results in nearly all cases, although in certain pastry and cake recipes a more accurate conversion is necessary to produce a balanced recipe.

Liquid measures

The millilitre has been used in this book and the following table gives a few examples.

Imperial	Approx ml to nearest whole figure	Recommended ml
$\frac{1}{4}$ pint	142	150 ml
$\frac{1}{2}$ pint	283	300 ml
$\frac{3}{4}$ pint	425	450 ml
1 pint	567	600 ml
$1\frac{1}{2}$ pints	851	900 ml
$1\frac{3}{4}$ pints	992	1000 ml (1 litre)

Can sizes

At present, cans are marked with the exact (usually to the nearest whole number) metric equivalent of the Imperial weight of the contents, so we have followed this practice when giving can sizes.

Oven temperatures

The table below gives recommended equivalents.

	°C	°F	Gas Mark
Very cool	110	225	$\frac{1}{4}$
	120	250	$\frac{1}{2}$
Cool	140	275	1
	150	300	2
Moderate	160	325	3
	180	350	4
Moderately hot	190	375	5
	200	400	6
Hot	220	425	7
	230	450	8
Very hot	240	475	9

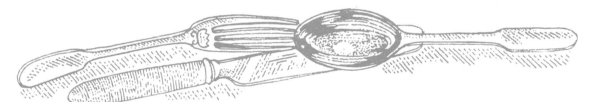

Notes for American and Australian users

In America the 8-oz measuring cup is used. In Australia metric measures are now used in conjunction with the standard 250-ml measuring cup. The Imperial pint, used in Britain and Australia, is 20 fl oz, while the American pint is 16 fl oz. It is important to remember that the Australian tablespoon differs from both the British and American tablespoons; the table below gives a comparison. The British standard tablespoon, which has been used throughout this book, holds 17.7 ml, the American 14.2 ml, and the Australian 20 ml. A teaspoon holds approximately 5 ml in all three countries.

British	American	Australian
1 teaspoon	1 teaspoon	1 teaspoon
1 tablespoon	1 tablespoon	1 tablespoon
2 tablespoons	3 tablespoons	2 tablespoons
$3\frac{1}{2}$ tablespoons	4 tablespoons	3 tablespoons
4 tablespoons	5 tablespoons	$3\frac{1}{2}$ tablespoons

An Imperial/American guide to solid and liquid measures

Solid measures

Imperial	American
1 lb butter or margarine	2 cups
1 lb flour	4 cups
1 lb granulated or castor sugar	2 cups
1 lb icing sugar	3 cups
8 oz rice	1 cup

Liquid measures

Imperial	American
$\frac{1}{4}$ pint liquid	$\frac{2}{3}$ cup liquid
$\frac{1}{2}$ pint	$1\frac{1}{4}$ cups
$\frac{3}{4}$ pint	2 cups
1 pint	$2\frac{1}{2}$ cups
$1\frac{1}{2}$ pints	$3\frac{3}{4}$ cups
2 pints	5 cups ($2\frac{1}{2}$ pints)

Introduction

A glass of smoke-filled **pastis**, a dish of those perfect, hard, little green olives that are the natural fruit of Provence, and a parcel of bright blue sea stretching as far as the human eye can reach – and then some – is my idea of a summer meal of perfection. At least, the humble beginnings of a summer meal that might continue, if I were marooned in one of the little fishing ports along the coast of sunny Provence, with a Provençal anchovy salad, made with salted anchovies, wine and olive oil, and spiked with fresh herbs and thin lemon slices. The whole is marinated until the anchovies are tender and soft, and the essence of the lemon and herbs has permeated the flesh of these delicious fish.

In Britain we can get salted anchovies by the piece or the quarter pound from little speciality shops in Soho, or buy them in large cans and use them as the occasion warrants. It is an easy task to wash away the salt in which they are packed, snip off the heads and tails, and gently prise the rose-tinted fillets from their bones. It is simplicity itself to place these fillets carefully in a bowl and douse them in equal quantities of olive oil and red wine. They are then flavoured, as the spirit moves you, with finely chopped shallots, onions or garlic, or a hint of all three, and a judicious sprinkling of finely chopped fresh parsley, chives or basil and, of course, several thin rounds of lemon.

Another cool, summery-tasting appetiser that I enjoy preparing is the Greek fish pâté called **taramasalata**. My more sophisticated, softer tasting version uses cream cheese for its creamy emulsion instead of the more traditional boiled potato or white bread. Taramasalata is an eastern cousin of Provençal **poutargue** – salted and smoked roe of tuna or grey mullet, sliced thinly and served as an *hors-d'oeuvre* with freshly ground black pepper, olive oil and lemon juice. **Taramasalata** uses smoked cod's roe rather than tuna or grey mullet and is quite delicious.

Freshly caught fish from the Gulf of Pampelonne, just thirty feet across the sands from the open-air barbecues where they are cooked, is one of the great delights of St. Tropez in the summer. Some of the little restaurants along the beach are beginning to do barbecued fish and shellfish appetisers for lunch, and can be tempted to carry this on to late-night suppers under the stars. Everything here is of optimum freshness. The vegetables – and even the wines served at one or two of these restaurants – come from the farms and vineyards located in the flatlands just behind the beach. A recent meal I enjoyed there began with a sumptious **salade niçoise** – tiny whole artichokes sliced with celery, onions, radishes, small green peppers, tomatoes, cucumber and lettuce, and garnished with black olives, quarters of hard-boiled egg, tuna fish and anchovies, dressed with a wine vinegar and olive oil dressing. This was followed by fresh sardines from the Gulf, brushed with a sauce of olive oil, lemon juice and fresh herbs, grilled over charcoal, and served with a dressing of melted butter and finely chopped tarragon. Melon and black coffee provided the finale to a perfect open-air meal.

Barbecued lobster makes a delectable first course, too, when split, enfolded in fresh sprigs of tarragon, basil and chervil, and grilled to succulent, pink-shelled perfection over the coals. I like to dribble olive oil and lemon juice on them during cooking and serve them simply with melted butter to which finely chopped herbs and a little lemon juice impart their own special flavours.

Hot and Cold Appetisers

There are almost countless numbers of appetisers, but the preparation of a large number of them requires the skill of a professional chef, to say nothing of a great amount of time and expensive ingredients.

Heading the list of simpler ones are oysters on the half-shell, six or nine freshly opened natives of Colchester or Whitstable, served on ice with coarse black pepper, and a wedge or two of lemon. Surround them with tiny sausages, piping hot, as they do in Northern France; or remove the oysters from their shells, roll them in fresh breadcrumbs and fry them in oil and butter. Serve immediately with a Bérnaise sauce, or more simply, with wedges of lemon.

I like, too, great oiled platters of smoked fish – salmon, sturgeon, trout and eel – or small cups of dressed crab, prawns and lobster served on individual trays of crushed ice with a choice of subtle sauces. And here a word of warning: don't have seafood sauces too pungent and sharp if fine wines accompany the first course, or are to follow. Better serve your fresh shellfish very plain and very cold, with perhaps a dash of lemon juice or a touch of **Crème Marie Rose**, freshly made mayonnaise and whipped cream in equal parts, enlivened by a dash of Tabasco, a little tomato ketchup and a hint of cognac.

But all of the above – no matter how choice – can be prepared without thought or attention on the part of the host or hostess. I much prefer, when dining out, to be given something a little more personal. Hot and cold appetisers – the sort that one often meets with in France as the beginning of a country meal – are the perfect answer here. For the most part they can be prepared ahead of time; they are often made of left-overs; and they can be added to or subtracted from to balance the rest of the meal. Why not try a popular French dish from the Mediterranean? **Caviar d'aubergines** (a chilled 'poor man's caviar'), while quite unlike its namesake, is quite delicious.

To make caviar d'aubergines: bake 1 or 2 large aubergines in a moderately hot oven (200°C, 400°F, Gas Mark 6) until soft – about 1 hour. Peel and chop 1 Spanish onion, 1 small green pepper, 4 tomatoes, 1 clove garlic and sauté them until golden in 6 to 8 tablespoons olive oil. Peel baked aubergine, chop its flesh finely and add to other ingredients; simmer vegetables gently, stirring from time to time, until excess moisture has evaporated and the mixture is fairly thick. Season to taste with salt and freshly ground black pepper and allow to cool. Just before serving, stir in 1 or 2 tablespoons each of dry white wine, olive oil and finely chopped parsley. Chill and serve with lemon wedges and thin slices of French bread.

Again, from Provence, comes the well-known hot appetiser, **petits pâtes à la Provençale** (shortcrust pastry rounds filled with minced cooked ham or veal flavoured with finely chopped anchovy, onion and garlic). I often serve these piping hot with drinks or with an inexpensive dry *rosé* wine on-the-rocks at cocktail parties. Try them, too, with tuna fish instead of veal. Delicious and different.

Mushrooms à la Grecque is one of my favourite ways of starting a meal. Try vegetables – cauliflower, carrots and beans – prepared in this way for a trio of vegetable appetisers that could lend freshness and flavour to a rustic meal. The secret here is to blanch the vegetables slightly before cooking them in wine. Be sure not to overcook them or they will be tasteless and soggy.

Haricots blancs en salade – this highly decorative country salad of dried white beans, with its hearty sauce flavoured with finely chopped onion, garlic, parsley and mustard, is garnished with anchovy fillets, tomato wedges and black olives for a Mediterranean effect.

A favourite hot appetiser for September dinner parties is **brochette de moules** – mussels steamed open with dry white wine, finely chopped shallots and herbs, skewered alternately with fat cubes of bacon, brushed with butter and cooked under the grill. Serve with lemon wedges, or better still, a Béarnaise sauce.

Salade de boeuf is another appetiser-salad favourite of mine. This is a wonderful way of making good use of left-over roast beef, but do be sure it is rare. **Salade de boeuf** also makes a good light luncheon dish or can double as one of the star turns for a buffet party.

Two of France's most celebrated restaurants – the Pyramide at Vienne and the Bonne Auberge at Antibes – make a speciality of serving course after course of hot and cold appetisers with great *panache*. At Antibes some people make their whole meal of these delicious *hors-d'oeuvre*. You, too, can make this an easy entertaining pattern for your own parties.

Tomato Salad 'Fines Herbes'

8 large ripe tomatoes
8 level tablespoons finely chopped parsley
4 level tablespoons finely chopped onion
1 level tablespoon finely chopped garlic
2 level tablespoons finely chopped basil
2 level tablespoons finely chopped tarragon
6-8 tablespoons olive oil
2-3 tablespoons wine vinegar
salt and freshly ground black pepper
Vinaigrette Sauce (see page 83)

1. Place large, firm, ripe tomatoes in boiling water for a few minutes. Peel and cut each tomato in even-sized thick slices. Re-form tomatoes and place in a rectangular or oval *hors-d'oeuvre* dish.

2. Mix the next 8 ingredients to form a thick, green, well-flavoured dressing. Sandwich three-quarters of the dressing carefully between layers of each tomato. Chill.

3. Dilute remaining dressing with a well-flavoured Vinaigrette Sauce; spoon over herb-stuffed tomatoes and serve.

Cucumber-stuffed Tomatoes

8 large ripe tomatoes
salt and freshly ground black pepper
½ large cucumber

DRESSING
6 tablespoons olive oil
6 tablespoons wine vinegar
salt and freshly ground black pepper
sugar

1. Cut tops off tomatoes and scoop out pulp and seeds. Sprinkle with salt and freshly ground black pepper. Turn upside down on a plate and chill.

2. Cut unpeeled cucumber into very thin slices. Place slices on a plate and salt them generously; cover with another plate and place a weight on top. Leave them for 2 hours, then rinse cucumber with cold water. Place in a clean towel and press to rid cucumber slices of all liquids.

11

3. Make a salad dressing with equal parts of olive oil and wine vinegar; flavour to taste with salt, freshly ground black pepper and a little sugar, and fold sliced cucumber into dressing.

4. To serve: turn tomato cases right side up; fill with cucumber and serve as an appetiser, or as an accompaniment to poached salmon.

Raw Spinach Salad with Bacon and Beans

450 g/1 lb cooked kidney or broad beans
6-8 tablespoons olive oil
3 tablespoons wine vinegar or
    lemon juice
1 level tablespoon each finely chopped fresh
    tarragon, basil and parsley
1-2 cloves garlic, finely chopped
salt and freshly ground black pepper
450 g/1 lb young spinach leaves, raw
1 small onion, thinly sliced
2 rashers well-cooked bacon, crumbled

1. Mix cooked beans with dressing made of olive oil and wine vinegar or lemon juice, and finely chopped herbs and garlic. Add salt and freshly ground black pepper, to taste.

2. Serve on tender young spinach leaves and garnish with onion rings and crumbled bacon.

Celeriac Salad

1 celery root
salted water
300 ml/½ pint well-flavoured mayonnaise
    (see page 89)
freshly ground black pepper
mustard, curry powder or paprika

1. Trim and wash celery root. Cut into matchstick-sized strips and blanch until tender in boiling salted water. Drain; cool and dry.

2. Dress with mayonnaise seasoned to taste with freshly ground black pepper and mustard, curry powder or paprika.

12

Russian Tomato Salad
Illustrated on page 25

4-8 ripe tomatoes
150 ml/¼ pint double cream, whipped
4-8 level tablespoons well-flavoured
  mayonnaise (see page 89)
1 level tablespoon freshly grated horseradish
¼ level teaspoon paprika
salt and freshly ground black pepper
lettuce leaves
4 level tablespoons finely chopped parsley
  or chives

1. Peel tomatoes and chill until ready to serve.

2. Combine whipped cream with mayonnaise,
grated horseradish and paprika, and season to
taste with salt and freshly ground black pepper.
Chill.

3. When ready to serve, place tomatoes on lettuce
leaves on individual salad plates and top with
dressing. Garnish with parsley or chives.

Vegetables with Aïoli Sauce

6 potatoes
6 baby marrows
450 g/1 lb new carrots
450 g/1 lb green beans
6 ripe tomatoes
salt and freshly ground black pepper
Aïoli Sauce (see page 89)

1. Peel potatoes and cut into 1-cm/½-inch cubes.
Wash and cut baby marrows, new carrots and
green beans into 1-cm/½-inch lengths.

2. Boil each vegetable separately until tender but
still quite firm. Do not overcook. Chill.

3. Seed and cut large fresh tomatoes into 1-cm/½-
inch cubes.

4. Arrange vegetables in colourful groups on a
large shallow serving dish. Sprinkle with salt and
freshly ground black pepper, to taste. Serve with
Aïoli Sauce.

Salade de Tomates à la Crème

12 ripe tomatoes
1 Spanish onion, finely chopped
6 tablespoons olive oil
2 tablespoons wine vinegar
salt and freshly ground black pepper
6 level tablespoons mayonnaise (see
  page 89)
4 level tablespoons double cream
2 level tablespoons chopped parsley

1. Cut tomatoes in slices and place on a dish.
Sprinkle with finely chopped onion.

2. Moisten with a simple dressing, made with
olive oil and wine vinegar seasoned with salt and
freshly ground black pepper.

3. Mix mayonnaise and cream, and cover tomatoes and onions. Sprinkle with parsley.

Sardine-stuffed Lemons

6 large fresh lemons
2 (120-g/4¼-oz) cans sardines or 1 (198-g/
  7-oz) can tuna fish
150 g/5 oz butter
prepared mustard
paprika
freshly ground black pepper
1 egg white, stiffly beaten
1 sprig fresh thyme, 1 bay leaf or small
  green leaf per lemon

1. Cut off tops of lemons; dig out pulp with a
small spoon. Remove pips and reserve pulp and
juice.

2. Mash sardines or tuna fish to a smooth paste
with butter and mustard, and season to taste with
paprika and freshly ground black pepper.

3. Stir in juice and pulp of lemons together with
stiffly beaten egg white. Correct seasoning and
stuff lemons with this mixture.

4. Chill. Top with a sprig of fresh thyme, a bay
leaf or a small green leaf, and serve in eggcups.

Spanish Vegetable Salad

1 Spanish onion
iced water
1 large cucumber
12 ripe tomatoes
6 level tablespoons dry French breadcrumbs
150 ml/¼ pint garlic-flavoured French
   Dressing (see Seafood Salad, page 14)
2 level tablespoons chopped basil, or chives,
   or a combination of the two

1. Peel and slice Spanish onion thinly and soak in iced water for 1 hour. Drain well. Slice cucumber thinly, but do not peel. Peel and slice tomatoes. Grate dry French bread to fine crumbs.

2. Prepare French Dressing, flavouring it with finely chopped garlic.

3. Arrange cucumber, tomatoes, onion and breadcrumbs in alternate layers in a glass salad bowl. Pour over a well-flavoured French dressing. Chill. Just before serving, sprinkle with chopped herbs.

Italian Vegetable Salad

Illustrated on page 26

4 tomatoes
wine vinegar
olive oil
salt and freshly ground black pepper
1 small cucumber
2 small green peppers
100 g/4 oz button mushrooms
2 level tablespoons finely chopped parsley
   lettuce
2 hard-boiled eggs

ITALIAN DRESSING
150 ml/¼ pint olive oil
4 anchovy fillets, finely chopped
juice of 1 large lemon
salt and freshly ground black pepper
1 level tablespoon capers

1. Quarter tomatoes and toss lightly in a small bowl with a little wine vinegar, olive oil, salt and freshly ground black pepper.

2. Peel cucumber and slice thinly. Place in a small bowl with a little wine vinegar, olive oil, salt and freshly ground black pepper.

3. Remove seeds and pith from green peppers. Slice into thin strips and place in a small bowl with the same dressing as above.

4. Wash and slice raw mushrooms into thin slices. Dress with a little wine vinegar and olive oil and add 1 tablespoon finely chopped parsley.

5. **To make Italian Dressing:** slightly warm 150 ml/¼ pint olive oil and add finely chopped anchovy fillets, mashing them with a fork until they are well blended with the oil. Add lemon juice and salt, freshly ground black pepper and capers, to taste.

6. Just before serving, assemble salads on a bed of lettuce in a large wooden bowl. Garnish with quartered hard-boiled eggs and sprinkle liberally with Italian Dressing.

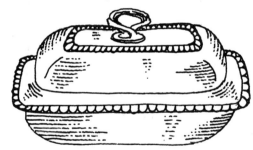

Haricots Verts 'en Aïoli'

450 g/1 lb green beans
6-8 level tablespoons Aïoli Sauce (see
   page 89)
freshly ground black pepper
3-4 level tablespoons finely chopped parsley

1. Cook beans in boiling salted water until tender – about 20 minutes. Drain well.

2. Mix while still warm with Aïoli Sauce. Toss well, season with salt and freshly ground black pepper, and chill.

3. Just before serving, toss well and sprinkle with finely chopped parsley.

13

Mushroom Salad with Chives *Serves 4 to 6*
Stuffed Tomatoes *Serves 4*
Seafood Salad *Serves 4*
Coeurs de Celéri en Salade *Serves 4*

14

Mushroom Salad with Chives
Illustrated on page 28

350 g/12 oz button mushrooms
juice of 1 lemon
8 tablespoons olive oil
salt and freshly ground black pepper
2 level tablespoons coarsely chopped chives
1 level tablespoon coarsely chopped parsley

1. Trim bottoms of mushroom stems; wash and dry mushrooms but do not peel.

2. Slice caps and arrange them in an *hors-d'oeuvre* dish or salad bowl. Pour well flavoured lemon and olive oil dressing over them.

3. Toss carefully, sprinkle with chopped chives and parsley, and chill in the refrigerator for 1 hour before serving.

Stuffed Tomatoes

8 large tomatoes
150 g/5 oz butter
6 level tablespoons chopped spring onions
2 cloves garlic, finely chopped
2 level tablespoons finely chopped parsley
225 g/8 oz cooked ham, finely chopped
8-12 level tablespoons shredded white bread
salt and freshly ground black pepper
dried breadcrumbs

1. Slice tops off tomatoes and scoop out interiors, being careful not to break cases. Chop pulp coarsely.

2. Melt 100 g/4 oz butter in a large thick-bottomed frying pan, and sauté onions, garlic, parsley, ham and tomato pulp until onions are soft. Add shredded white bread which you have soaked in water and squeezed relatively dry. Season with salt and freshly ground black pepper.

3. Stuff tomato cases with this mixture. Top with breadcrumbs, dot with remaining butter and bake in a moderate oven (180°C, 350°F, Gas Mark 4) for 20 minutes. Serve stuffed tomatoes either hot or cold.

Seafood Salad

1 soft-leaved lettuce, washed and chilled
1 Cos lettuce, washed and chilled
225 g/8 oz cooked prawns
225 g/8 oz cooked lobster meat
225 g/8 oz cooked white fish
225 g/8 oz cooked crabmeat
4 ripe tomatoes
8 large black olives

FRENCH DRESSING
1 tablespoon lemon juice
1-2 tablespoons wine vinegar
¼ teaspoon dry mustard
coarse salt and freshly ground black pepper
6-8 tablespoons olive oil

1. Line salad bowl with lettuce and Cos leaves. Arrange prawns, lobster, white fish and crabmeat, cut in cubes, on bed of salad greens. Garnish with wedges of ripe tomato and black olives.

2. To make French Dressing: mix together lemon juice, wine vinegar and dry mustard, and season to taste with coarse salt and freshly ground black pepper. Add olive oil and beat with a fork until the mixture emulsifies.

Coeurs de Celéri en Salade

2 heads celery
1 chicken stock cube
1 level tablespoon salt
300 ml/½ pint well-flavoured Vinaigrette
    Sauce (see page 83)
½ level teaspoon paprika
cayenne
150 ml/¼ pint double cream
4 hard-boiled eggs
4 level tablespoons finely chopped parsley

1. Trim heads of celery, cutting off top third of branches and outside stalks. Cut each head in half; put celery in a saucepan with trimmings, chicken stock cube and salt. Cover with cold water and bring slowly to the boil. Simmer for 10 minutes, remove from heat and leave in hot water for 5 minutes. Drain and cool.

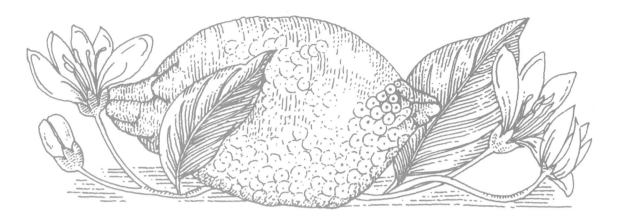

2. Arrange celery in a flat serving dish. Spoon over half of the Vinaigrette Sauce and allow celery to marinate in this mixture for at least 1 hour.

3. Combine remaining Vinaigrette Sauce with paprika, a pinch of cayenne and the double cream; mix well.

4. Separate yolks from whites of eggs and rub each separately through a wire sieve.

5. To serve: place blanched celery hearts on a serving dish. Cover each celery half with dressing; garnish one-third of each portion with sieved egg white, one-third with sieved egg yolk, and remaining third with finely chopped parsley. Serve immediately.

Appetiser Salad Marly

225 g/8 oz green asparagus tips, cooked
100 g/4 oz button mushrooms
4-6 tomatoes

SAUCE MARLY
1 level tablespoon Dijon mustard
175 ml/6 fl oz thick cream
juice of $\frac{1}{2}$ lemon
salt and freshly ground black pepper
few drops of vinegar

1. Arrange cooked and drained asparagus tips on a long dish. Slice raw mushrooms thinly on top. Cut

tomatoes into wedges and arrange around dish. Pour Sauce Marly over centre of dish.

2. To make Sauce Marly: combine mustard, cream and lemon juice, and season to taste with salt, freshly ground black pepper and vinegar.

Smoked Cod's Roe Mousse

1 jar smoked cod's roe (about 175 g/6 oz)
1$\frac{1}{2}$ (85-g/3-oz) packets cream cheese
$\frac{1}{4}$ Spanish onion, grated
1-2 cloves garlic, mashed
olive oil
juice of 1 lemon
1 tablespoon finely chopped parsley
green olives
butter
hot toast

1. Place cod's roe in a mortar. Add cream cheese and pound mixture to a smooth paste.

2. Stir in onion and garlic. Then add enough olive oil and lemon juice (alternately a little at a time) stirring well until mixture acquires a smooth, uniform consistency. Strain through a fine sieve. (The above can be done in an electric blender, in which case the mixture does not need to be sieved.)

3. Serve in a salad bowl, sprinkled with finely chopped parsley and garnished with green olives. Serve with butter and hot toast.

16

Frozen Asparagus Tips with Prosciutto

1 (227-g/8-oz) packet frozen asparagus tips,

**thin slices of prosciutto poached
butter
4 level tablespoons double cream
4 level tablespoons freshly grated Parmesan
cheese**

1. Wrap 2 poached asparagus tips in each slice of *prosciutto*. Fasten with wooden cocktail sticks.

2. Arrange bundles in a well-buttered ovenproof dish, and sprinkle with double cream, freshly grated Parmesan and 50 g/2 oz butter, diced. Bake in a moderately hot oven (200°C, 400°F, Gas Mark 6) for 5 minutes.

3. Melt 50 g/2 oz butter; pour over asparagus bundles and serve immediately.

Fresh Asparagus Hollandaise

1 bunch fresh asparagus

HOLLANDAISE SAUCE
**lemon juice
1 tablespoon cold water
salt and white pepper
225 g/8 oz softened butter
4 egg yolks**

1. **To boil asparagus:** select a deep, narrow pan in which the asparagus stalks can stand upright, and pour in boiling water to just under the tips; in this way, the stalks can cook in water and the tender heads can cook in steam. Simmer gently – about 10 to 15 minutes from the time the water comes to the boil again after immersion is just about right. Slender stalks will take less time.

2. **To steam asparagus:** lay asparagus stalks flat in a *gratin* dish; add 4 tablespoons chicken stock or water, 4 tablespoons butter, and salt and freshly ground black pepper, to taste. Place *gratin* dish in the top of a double steamer over boiling water (or on a trivet or brick to hold *gratin* dish over water

in a large saucepan); cover pan and steam for 15 to 20 minutes, or until tender.

3. **To make Hollandaise Sauce:** combine 1 teaspoon of lemon juice, water and a pinch each of salt and white pepper in the top of a double saucepan or *bain-marie*. Divide butter into 4 equal pieces. Add the egg yolks and a quarter of the butter to the liquid in the saucepan, and stir the mixture rapidly and constantly with a wire whisk over hot, but not boiling, water until the butter is melted and the mixture begins to thicken. Add the second piece of butter and continue whisking. As the mixture thickens and the second piece of butter melts, add the third piece of butter, stirring from the bottom of the pan until it is melted. Be careful not to allow the water over which the sauce is cooking to boil at any time. Add rest of butter, beating until it melts and is incorporated in the sauce. Remove top part of saucepan from heat and continue to beat for 2 to 3 minutes. Replace saucepan over hot, but not boiling, water for 2 minutes more, beating constantly. By this time the emulsion should have formed and your sauce will be rich and creamy. 'Finish' sauce with a few drops of lemon juice. Strain and serve. If at any time in the operation the mixture should curdle, beat in 1 or 2 tablespoons cold water to rebind the emulsion.

4. Drain boiled or steamed asparagus and serve with Hollandaise Sauce.

Mushrooms in Mustard

**450 g/1 lb button mushrooms
juice of 1 lemon
8 tablespoons olive oil
6 black peppercorns
2 bay leaves
1-2 level tablespoons Dijon mustard
salt
2-3 level tablespoons finely chopped parsley**

1. Wash and drain mushrooms. Trim ends of stems with a sharp knife and cut mushrooms in halves or quarters.

2. Marinate in lemon juice and olive oil with

peppercorns and bay leaves for at least 8 hours. Drain mushrooms (reserving marinade juices) and arrange them in an *hors-d'oeuvre* dish.

3. To make mustard sauce: combine 4 to 6 tablespoons marinade juices with Dijon mustard in a small jar, and shake until well blended. Add salt and a little more lemon juice or olive oil if necessary.

4. Pour sauce over mushrooms. Sprinkle with finely chopped parsley.

Artichokes with Green Mayonnaise

4 artichokes
salt
juice of ½ lemon

GREEN MAYONNAISE
300 ml/½ pint well-flavoured mayonnaise (see page 89)
1 handful each sprigs of watercress, parsley and chervil
2 level tablespoons finely chopped watercress leaves
2 level tablespoons finely chopped chervil
4 level tablespoons finely chopped parsley
2 level tablespoons finely chopped tarragon leaves
lemon juice
freshly ground black pepper

1. Remove tough outer leaves of artichokes and trim tops of inner leaves. Trim the base and stem of each artichoke with a sharp knife.

2. Cook until tender – 30 to 40 minutes – in a large quantity of salted boiling water to which you have added the juice of ½ lemon. Artichokes are ready when a leaf pulls out easily. When cooked, turn artichokes upside down to drain.

3. To make Green Mayonnaise: wash sprigs of watercress, parsley and chervil. Pick them over carefully and put them in a saucepan with a little salted boiling water. Allow greens to boil for 6 to 7 minutes; drain and press as dry as possible. Pound greens in a mortar. Rub through a fine

sieve and add green purée to mayonnaise. Whirl green mayonnaise and finely chopped watercress leaves and herbs in an electric blender, or blend well with a whisk. Add lemon juice, salt and freshly ground black pepper, to taste.

4. Serve artichokes with Green Mayonnaise.

Italian Antipasto Platter
Illustrated on page 27

1 lettuce
4 tomatoes, cut in wedges
4 fennel, cut in wedges
1 (198-g/7-oz) can tuna fish or 2 (120-g/4¼-oz) cans sardines
1 (198-g/7-oz) can artichokes in oil or brine
8 slices Italian salami
4 slices mortadella or prosciutto
8 radishes
8 black olives
2 level tablespoons finely chopped parsley or capers

ITALIAN DRESSING
150 ml/¼ pint olive oil
2 anchovy fillets, finely chopped
lemon juice
salt and freshly ground black pepper
capers

1. To make Italian dressing: warm olive oil slightly and add anchovy fillets, finely chopped, mashing them with a fork until they are well blended with the oil. Add lemon juice and salt, pepper and capers, to taste.

2. Wash and trim lettuce. Dry leaves throughly. Cut tomatoes into wedges and toss lightly in Italian dressing. Clean and trim fennel and cut into thin wedges; toss lightly in dressing. Drain oil from tuna fish (or sardines); drain oil from artichokes. Chill vegetables.

3. Arrange lettuce leaves on a large serving dish. Place sliced meats, fish, vegetables, radishes and black olives in colourful groups on lettuce. Sprinkle with finely chopped parsley or capers. Serve with crusty bread and butter.

Egg Appetisers

How many of us today relegate the egg to the everyday breakfast basics of fried, boiled, poached or scrambled? Omelettes, soufflés and quiches use eggs to perfection to introduce a lunch or dinner menu (see Smoked Salmon Quiche, page 51). Ring the changes on the basic omelette by adding diced sautéed potatoes, courgettes or aubergines. Even scrambled eggs can make their mark as a first course of distinction. I remember a remarkable luncheon at the elegant Plaza Athénée in Paris which started off with a delicious version of scrambled eggs (3 eggs per person cooked in butter until soft and moist) mixed with diced truffles and asparagus, piled into a golden *croustade* of flaky pastry garnished with individual moulds of ham mousse and asparagus tips. Elegant and different, you'll agree. And yet, except for the diced truffles and the ham mousse, not too difficult or extravagant to make.

Taking a leaf from the Plaza Athénée's book, I have often served small hot pastry cases filled just before serving with scrambled eggs, lightly flavoured with a little grated Parmesan and tossed with diced ham and mushrooms, simmered in butter. Try this, too, with thin slivers of sliced smoked salmon or flaked smoked trout and sliced radishes.

Oeufs moulés was a fashionable first course egg in nineteenth century France. Nothing more nor less than an egg baked in a *dariole* mould and then turned out before serving, these little egg turrets make a decorative first course today, especially if served with an appropriate sauce and placed in individual pastry cases, cooked artichoke hearts, mushroom caps or tomato cases.

Here again, the method is simplicity itself: butter individual *dariole* moulds generously. Break an egg into each mould; place moulds in a tin of hot water and cook in a moderate oven (180°C, 350°F, Gas Mark 4) for 15 minutes. The insides of the moulds can be sprinkled with finely chopped parsley, finely chopped chives blanched in boiling water, or finely chopped mushrooms simmered in butter.

To serve: turn out moulds into individual pastry cases and pour over any one of the three following sauces.

1. A purée of peeled, seeded and chopped tomatoes softened in butter with a hint of finely chopped shallot, thyme, salt and freshly ground black pepper.

2. A purée of poached artichoke hearts enriched with chicken *velouté* sauce and double cream.

3. A purée of poached asparagus tips enriched with chicken *velouté* and cream.

Or serve each **oeuf moulé** on a base of poached artichoke hearts, baked mushroom caps or tomato cases, and mask egg with a little well-flavoured Béchamel or Hollandaise sauce.

Stuffed Eggs with Green Mayonnaise

4-6 hard-boiled eggs
6 level tablespoons pounded buttered
    shrimps
6 level tablespoons mayonnaise (see page 89)
lemon juice
300-450 ml/½-¾ pint Green Mayonnaise (see
    Artichokes with Green Mayonnaise,
    page 17)
3 level tablespoons finely chopped fresh herbs

1. Shell hard-boiled eggs and cut them in half lengthwise. Remove yolks and mash them to a smooth thick paste with pounded buttered shrimps, mayonnaise and lemon juice, to taste.

2. Stuff each egg white with shrimp mixture, piling it up to re-form egg shape.

3. Arrange stuffed eggs on a bed of Green Mayonnaise in an *hors-d'oeuvre* dish. Sprinkle with finely chopped herbs.

Eggs in Aspic

Madeira Aspic (see Basic Meat Aspic,
    page 84)
8 fresh tarragon leaves
1 slice cooked ham, cut en julienne
4 poached eggs
2 level tablespoons each cooked peas, diced
    cooked turnip and diced cooked carrot
    (optional)

1. Coat the bottom of small individual moulds with Madeira Aspic; allow to set.

2. Pour boiling water over tarragon leaves; dry and arrange on aspic. Place 2 to 4 thin strips of ham across leaves, and dribble a little aspic over them to hold them in place.

3. Trim poached eggs with scissors and place in mould. Pour aspic over them to cover. Garnish, if desired, with cold cooked peas and diced cooked turnip and carrot. Cover with aspic. Chill. Unmould just before serving.

Oeufs en Cocotte

19

A popular first course today. Butter individual *cocottes* or soufflé dishes, break 1 or 2 eggs into each, flavour the eggs to taste with salt and freshly ground black pepper, cover each egg with a little hot cream, and bake in a preheated moderate oven (160°C to 180°C, 325°F to 350°F, Gas Mark 3 to 4) for 5 to 8 minutes, until the whites just begin to set and the yolks are still runny. The variations on this simple dish are infinite. I like the following:

1. Lightly sauté 4 to 6 tablespoons of diced chicken liver, Italian sausage or cooked ham in a little butter. Season generously with salt and freshly ground black pepper and divide among 4 to 6 individual ovenproof dishes or *cocottes*.

2. Sprinkle 1 or 2 eggs with a little finely grated cheese before adding 1 tablespoon double cream to each dish. Bake as above.

3. Spread a bed of creamed spinach in each ramekin or *cocotte*; add 1 or 2 eggs and 1 tablespoon double cream, to each dish. Bake as above and serve with a little tomato sauce.

Poached Eggs Hollandaise

1 recipe fingertip pastry (see Provençal
    Tomato and Onion Tart, page 54)
4 poached eggs
salt and freshly ground black pepper
butter
150 ml/¼ pint Hollandaise Sauce (see Fresh
    Asparagus Hollandaise, page 16)

1. Bake 4 individual pastry cases; remove from tins.

2. Place 1 poached egg in each case; season to taste with salt and freshly ground black pepper, and dot with butter. Warm through for a few minutes in a moderately hot oven (190°C, 375°F, Gas Mark 5).

3. Top each egg with 2 tablespoons Hollandaise Sauce and serve immediately.

20

Provençal Stuffed Eggs 'à la Tapénade'

8-10 black olives, stoned
4-5 anchovy fillets
4-5 level tablespoons tuna fish
1-2 level teaspoons Dijon mustard
2 tablespoons chopped capers
4-6 tablespoons olive oil
1 tablespoon cognac
freshly ground black pepper
4-6 hard-boiled eggs
finely chopped parsley
lettuce leaves
black olives for garnish

1. Pound stoned black olives, anchovy fillets and tuna fish in a mortar with mustard and capers. When the mixture has been blended to a smooth paste, put it through a fine sieve and whisk olive oil into it. Add cognac, and season to taste with freshly ground black pepper.

2. Cut hard-boiled eggs in half lengthwise and remove yolks. Blend yolks with *tapénade* mixture, adding a little more olive oil if necessary. Pipe egg hollows with mixture; sprinkle with finely chopped parsley and serve, garnished with lettuce leaves and black olives.

Note: The *tapénade* mixture keeps well in a covered jar and is excellent as a highly flavoured canapé spread.

Cold Oeufs Saumonées en Croûte

6 round rolls
butter
12 eggs
2 thin slices smoked salmon
6 level tablespoons double cream
salt and freshly ground black pepper
3 level tablespoons finely chopped parsley

1. Slice tops off rolls and pull out interiors of rolls with your fingers. Brush rolls inside and out with melted butter and bake in a moderate oven (180°C, 350°F, Gas Mark 4) until golden brown. Cool.

2. Mix eggs slightly until whites and yolks are well mixed, but do not beat them.

3. Cut thin slices of smoked salmon into thin strips and heat for a moment in 2 tablespoons butter.

4. Add eggs and cook, stirring constantly, over low heat. As eggs begin to set, add another 2 tablespoons butter and the cream. Season to taste with salt and freshly ground black pepper. Cool.

5. Stuff rolls with scrambled egg mixture and sprinkle with finely chopped parsley.

Oeufs Bénédictine

4 eggs
4 slices cooked ham
butter
4 slices white bread
150 ml/$\frac{1}{4}$ pint Hollandaise Sauce (see Fresh Asparagus Hollandaise, page 16)

1. Poach eggs and keep warm.

2. Cut 4 rounds of sliced ham just large enough to fit individual egg dishes. Warm in butter.

3. Toast bread and cut rounds of the same size. Butter toast rounds and place 1 in each heated egg dish.

4. Cover each round with warmed ham and top with a poached egg. Spoon over Hollandaise Sauce and serve immediately.

Surprise Eggs

4 eggs
8 level tablespoons grated Parmesan cheese
salt and white pepper
butter
4 level tablespoons double cream

1. Separate eggs. Beat the whites very stiff; add half the fully grated Parmesan and salt and white pepper, to taste. Mix well.

2. Butter individual ramekins or *cocottes*, and spoon an egg white into each. Use rather large dishes, as egg whites tend to rise like a soufflé. Make a depression with the back of your spoon for each egg yolk.

3. Place yolks in hollows (1 to each ramekin); cover each yolk with 1 tablespoon cream, and sprinkle with remaining grated cheese.

4. Bake in a hot oven (230°C, 450°F, Gas Mark 8) for 8 to 10 minutes.

Baked Eggs in Tomato Cups

4 large tomatoes
salt and freshly ground black pepper
4 eggs
butter

HOT CURRY SAUCE
2 level tablespoons butter
2 level tablespoons flour
150 ml/¼ pint milk
150 ml/¼ pint single cream
salt and white pepper
1 level teaspoon curry powder

1. Cut tops from tomatoes, remove pulp, and drain. Season insides of tomato cases with salt and a little freshly ground black pepper. Break an egg into each tomato case; dot with butter, and season with salt and freshly ground black pepper.

2. Bake in individual baking dishes in a moderately hot oven (190°C, 375°F, Gas Mark 5) until the eggs are firm. Serve topped with Hot Curry Sauce.

3. **To make Hot Curry Sauce:** melt butter in a thick-bottomed saucepan. Add flour and cook, stirring constantly, until well blended. Add milk and cream slowly, stirring constantly. Season to taste with salt, white pepper and curry powder. Cover and simmer gently for 8 minutes.

Scrambled Eggs

21

5 large eggs
salt and freshly ground black pepper
butter
6 level tablespoons double cream

1. Break eggs into a bowl and season to taste with salt and freshly ground black pepper. Mix eggs lightly with a fork, but do not beat them.

2. Heat 4 level tablespoons butter in the pan until it is sizzling but has not changed colour. Pour eggs into pan. Allow them to set slightly; then stir them constantly with a wooden spoon, running edge of spoon round the pan and drawing the eggs into the centre. Cook until creamy.

3. Then, with a wire whisk, whip double cream and a little diced butter into egg mixture until eggs are fluffy. Serve immediately on a hot plate.

Note: Good scrambled eggs need care and attention. Always heat the pan before adding butter. Use plenty of butter and make sure it is hot (but not coloured) before adding the eggs.

Scrambled Eggs with Cheese
Combine beaten eggs with grated Gruyère, Parmesan and double cream, to taste. Cook as in basic recipe above.

Scrambled Eggs with Buttered Shrimps
Warm shrimps through in their butter and fold into scrambled eggs cooked as in basic recipe.

Scrambled Eggs with Mushrooms
Sauté thinly sliced button mushrooms in butter until soft. Season generously with salt and freshly ground pepper, and fold into scrambled eggs when they are half cooked. Continue to cook as in basic recipe above. Garnish with sautéed mushroom caps.

Scrambled Eggs with Artichokes
Dice cooked artichoke hearts. Toss in butter, season generously with salt and freshly ground black pepper, and fold into scrambled eggs when they are half cooked. Continue to cook in basic recipe. Garnish with finely chopped parsley.

22

Scrambled Eggs Provençale

Illustrated on page 28

8 anchovy fillets
4 slices white bread
butter
olive oil
8 eggs
salt and freshly ground black pepper
black olives
cayenne
2 tablespoons finely chopped parsley

1. Heat the oven.

2. Slice the anchovy fillets in half lengthwise.

3. Cut the bread into rounds about 7.5 cm/3 inches in diameter and sauté lightly in a little butter and olive oil until just golden. Place on a baking sheet and put into the oven to keep warm.

4. Break the eggs into a mixing bowl; add salt, freshly ground black pepper and cayenne to taste, and mix lightly. Scramble the eggs in butter and olive oil.

5. Spoon the scrambled eggs on to the fried toast rounds and garnish with a lattice-work of thin anchovy strips, halved black olives and finely chopped parsley.

Scrambled Egg Croustades

1 recipe shortcrust pastry (see page 90)
12 eggs
6 level tablespoons butter
100 g/4 oz cooked ham, diced
6 button mushrooms, quartered and
   sautéed in butter

1. Line individual *brioche* moulds thinly with pastry and bake until golden. Keep warm.

2. Scramble eggs (3 per person) in butter until creamy but still quite moist. Toss with diced cooked ham and sautéed mushrooms.

3. Fill pastry cases and serve immediately.

Variation: Bake twice as many pastry cases as you will need. Pile eggs, ham and mushrooms high in half of the cases and top with remaining cases, inverted to form pastry covers.

Baked Eggs and Bacon

8 eggs
4-6 tablespoons diced Cheddar cheese
4 rashers bacon, grilled and diced
salt and freshly ground black pepper
8 tablespoons double cream

1. Butter 4 individual *cocottes* or soufflé dishes; sprinkle a quarter of the diced cheese and diced grilled bacon over the bottom of each dish. Break 2 eggs into each dish.

2. Season to taste with salt and freshly ground black pepper, and top with 2 tablespoons double cream.

3. Bake in a moderate oven (180°C, 350°F, Gas Mark 4) for 15 minutes, or until egg whites are firm.

Deep-fried Eggs in Pastry

4-6 eggs
salt and freshly ground black pepper
puff pastry (see page 90)
2 egg yolks, well beaten
dried breadcrumbs
fat for deep-frying

1. Soft-boil eggs and place them in cold water. Shell eggs carefully, and sprinkle to taste with salt and freshly ground black pepper.

2. Roll out pastry very thinly and cut out oblong-shaped pieces large enough to enfold each egg. Wrap each egg in pastry, sealing the joins with a little beaten egg. Trim superfluous pastry edges with scissors, making sure it is not too thick in any one part.

3. When ready to serve: brush eggs with beaten egg yolks; toss them in fine breadcrumbs and fry them in hot fat until golden brown. Drain well and serve immediately.

Basic Omelette

5 large eggs
salt and freshly ground black pepper
1 tablespoon water
2 level tablespoons butter
4 level tablespoons whipped egg white
freshly grated Gruyère or Parmesan cheese

1. Break eggs into a bowl and season to taste with salt and freshly ground black pepper. Heat an omelette pan gradually on a medium heat until it is hot enough to make butter sizzle on contact. Add water to eggs and beat with a fork or wire whisk just enough to mix yolks and whites. Add butter to heated pan and shake until butter coats bottom of pan evenly. When butter is sizzling, pour in the beaten eggs all at once.

2. Quickly stir eggs for a second or two in the pan to assure even cooking just as you would for scrambled eggs. Then, if you want your omelette to be supremely light, stir in 2 tablespoons whipped egg white and a sprinkling of freshly grated Gruyère or Parmesan – not enough to give it a cheesy flavour, but just enough to intensify the eggy taste of your omelette.

3. And now is the time to start working: as eggs begin to set, lift edges with a fork or palette knife so that the liquid can run under. Repeat until liquid is all used up but the eggs are still moist and soft, keeping eggs from sticking by shaking pan during the above operation.

4. Remove eggs from heat and, with one movement, slide the omelette towards the handle. When a third of the omelette has slid up the rounded edge of the pan, fold this quickly towards the centre with your palette knife. Raise the handle of the pan and slide opposite edge of omelette one-third up the side farthest away from the handle. Hold a heated serving dish under the pan, and as the rim of the omelette touches the dish, raise the handle more and more, until the pan is turned upside down and your oval-shaped, lightly browned omelette rests on the dish.
French chefs usually 'finish' their omelettes by skimming the surface lightly with a knob of butter on the point of a knife. Serve immediately.

After one or two tries to achieve your cook's *tour de main*, you should be able to produce a delicious omelette every time, golden on the outside and as juicy as you could wish inside.

24

Anchovy Omelette

4-6 large eggs
1 tablespoon water
4-6 anchovy fillets, finely chopped
2 level tablespoons finely chopped parsley
1 tomato, peeled, seeded and chopped
olive oil
2 level tablespoons freshly grated Gruyère
** cheese**
butter

1. Beat eggs with water until well mixed. Add chopped anchovy fillets, parsley and tomato.

2. Heat olive oil until sizzling in a preheated omelette pan. Remove pan from heat and pour in egg mixture. Return to heat and, shaking pan with one hand, stir egg mixture with fork in the other hand until eggs just begin to set. Sprinkle with freshly grated Gruyère and quickly stir eggs with a wide circular motion, shaking pan constantly to keep omelette from sticking.

3. When eggs are set but surface is still moist, roll omelette on to a hot plate by tilting pan, starting it away from edge at one side with a fork and letting it roll over itself. Pick up a small piece of butter on the point of a sharp knife and rub it over omelette. Serve immediately.

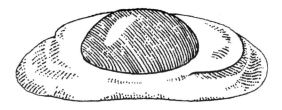

Omelette Provençale

2 tomatoes, peeled, seeded and finely
** chopped**
1 clove garlic, finely chopped
1 small onion, finely chopped
8 sprigs fresh parsley, chopped
2 sprigs fresh tarragon, chopped
salt and freshly ground black pepper
2 tablespoons olive oil
4 eggs
2 level tablespoons butter

1. Combine finely chopped tomatoes, garlic, onion, parsley and tarragon. Season with salt and freshly ground black pepper, and sauté in olive oil in a frying pan for about 10 minutes. Keep warm.

2. Beat eggs lightly, season with salt and pepper, and cook in butter as for Basic Omelette (see page 23). When eggs are still soft, spread vegetables in centre, fold omelette and serve at once on a heated dish.

Omelette Bénédictine

This is an excellent luncheon omelette if you have left-over *brandade de morue*.

4-6 large eggs
1 tablespoon water
butter or olive oil
6-8 level tablespoons Brandade de Morue
** (see page 76)**

CREAM SAUCE
2 level tablespoons butter
2 level tablespoons flour
150 ml/$\frac{1}{4}$ pint dry white wine
150 ml/$\frac{1}{4}$ pint double cream
salt and freshly ground black pepper

1. Beat eggs with water until well mixed.

2. Heat butter or olive oil until sizzling in a preheated omelette pan. Remove pan from heat and pour in egg mixture. Return to heat and, shaking pan with one hand, stir egg mixture with fork in the other hand until eggs just begin to set.

3. When eggs are still soft, spread warmed *brandade de morue* over centre. Fold omelette; transfer to a heated dish, pour Cream Sauce over it and serve at once.

4. To make Cream Sauce: melt butter in the top of a double saucepan; stir in flour and cook, stirring constantly, until smooth. Add dry white wine and double cream, and stir until boiling. Reduce heat and cook, stirring from time to time, until smooth. Season to taste with salt and freshly ground black pepper.

Russian Tomato Salad (see page 12)
Artichokes with Mustard Mayonnaise (see page 30)

Italian Antipasto Platter (see page 17)
Italian Vegetable Salad (see page 13)

Scrambled Eggs Provençale (see page 22)

Mushroom Salad with Chives (see page 14)

Cooked Appetisers from around the World

Asparagus Polonaise

1 kg/2 lb asparagus
pinch of sugar
salt and freshly ground black pepper
2 level tablespoons butter

POLONAISE SAUCE
100 g/4 oz butter
75 g/3 oz light breadcrumbs
2 hard-boiled eggs, finely chopped
2 level tablespoons finely chopped chives

1. Wash and trim asparagus. Lay it flat in a shallow saucepan and cook, covered, in a small amount of boiling water to which you have added sugar, salt, freshly ground black pepper and butter, until just tender – 10 to 15 minutes.

2. Drain asparagus and place on serving dish. Spoon Polonaise Sauce over it and serve immediately.

3. **To make Polonaise Sauce:** melt butter in a saucepan. Add breadcrumbs and sauté gently until light brown, then add finely chopped hard-boiled eggs and chives.

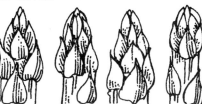

Italian Baked Asparagus

450 g/1 lb uncooked asparagus spears
4 level tablespoons butter
4 level tablespoons finely chopped onion
4 level tablespoons finely chopped celery
2 level tablespoons freshly grated Parmesan
   cheese
2 level tablespoons fresh breadcrumbs
4 canned Italian peeled tomatoes, diced
salt and freshly ground black pepper
pinch of oregano
pinch of thyme

1. Melt butter in the bottom of a rectangular baking dish. Line bottom with asparagus spears; sprinkle with finely chopped onion and celery, grated cheese and breadcrumbs and diced canned tomatoes, and season to taste with salt, pepper, oregano and thyme.

2. Cover and bake in a moderately hot oven (190°C, 375°F, Gas Mark 5) for about 45 minutes.

Délices au Gruyère

4 level tablespoons butter
flour
450 ml/¾ pint boiling milk
8 level tablespoons freshly grated Gruyère
   cheese
4 level tablespoons freshly grated Parmesan
   cheese
freshly grated nutmeg
2 egg yolks
salt and freshly ground black pepper
1 egg beaten with 2 tablespoons milk and
   1 tablespoon olive oil
fresh breadcrumbs
oil for frying

1. Melt butter in the top of a double saucepan. Stir in 4 level tablespoons flour and cook over water, stirring continuously with a wooden spoon, until smooth. Pour in boiling milk and mix with a whisk to make a thick sauce.

2. Simmer sauce for a few minutes longer. Add grated Gruyère and Parmesan and a little grated nutmeg, and continue cooking, stirring continuously, until cheese is completely blended.

3. Remove sauce from heat. Stir in egg yolks; season to taste with salt and freshly ground black pepper, and more nutmeg if desired. Continue to cook over water, stirring continuously, for 2 or 3 minutes, being careful not to let mixture boil. Spread in a rectangular baking tin and allow to cool. Cover with paper or foil and chill in refrigerator for 3 hours, or until needed.

4. Just before serving, cut into rectangles; flour lightly and dip in egg beaten with milk and olive oil. Drain, roll in fresh breadcrumbs and fry in hot oil until golden. Serve immediately.

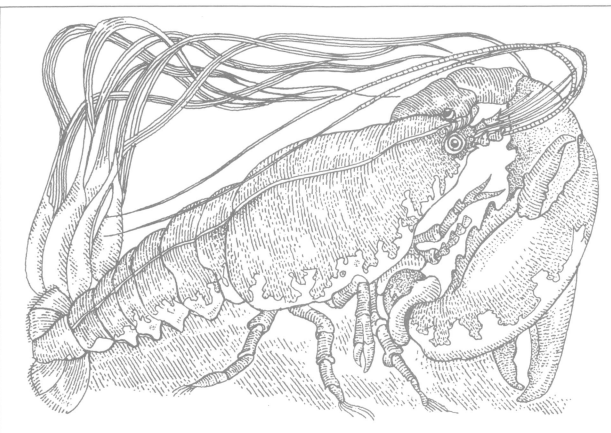

Bouillabaisse Salad 'Four Seasons'

2 lobsters (about 1 kg/2 lb each)
2 dozen mussels
16 prawns
450 g/1 lb crabmeat
75 g/3 oz chopped celery
1 lettuce
2 or 3 tomatoes, very thinly sliced
1 hard-boiled egg, finely chopped

DRESSING
250 ml/8 fl oz olive oil
175 ml/6 fl oz wine vinegar
4 tablespoons fish stock (reduced liquid in which shellfish were cooked, or canned clam juice)
½ Spanish onion, finely chopped
2 tablespoons dry white wine
1 tablespoon finely chopped chives
salt and freshly ground white pepper

1. All shellfish must be cooked and cooled before preparing salad.

2. In a shallow salad bowl, arrange celery, lobster and crabmeat in centre of bed of lettuce. Place mussels, prawns and sliced tomatoes alternately around edge of bowl.

3. To make the dressing: mix oil, vinegar, fish stock, onion, dry white wine and finely chopped chives. Season to taste with salt and freshly ground white pepper, and pour over salad.

4. Garnish with chopped egg and serve.

Artichokes with Mustard Mayonnaise
Illustrated on page 25

1. With a strong, sharp knife, slice all the leaves off level with the tips of the shortest ones. Strip away any tough outer leaves. Trim base and stem.

2. With a sharp-edged teaspoon, scoop and scrape out the fuzzy chokes, taking care not to leave a single fibre. Remember that these fibres are called 'chokes' for a very good reason.

3. While you are working on the artichoke, keep dipping it into a bowl of water heavily acidulated with lemon juice each time you cut open a fresh surface to prevent it turning brown. The artichoke contains peroxides and oxidising enzymes which cause it – and any steel utensil used with it – to discolour very quickly when exposed to the air. This is not dangerous, but it makes the artichoke look unattractive and spoils its flavour.

4. To a large pan of water add a handful of salt and some lemon juice (or a squeezed-out lemon half). Bring to the boil.

5. Immerse artichokes and simmer for 30 to 40 minutes, or until you can pull a leaf out easily.

6. Lift out artichokes and leave them to drain standing on their heads in a colander.

MUSTARD MAYONNAISE
2 egg yolks
1-2 level teaspoons Dijon mustard
salt and freshly ground black pepper
lemon juice
300 ml/½ pint olive oil

1. Have all ingredients at room temperature before you start. This is important: eggs straight from the refrigerator and cloudy olive oil are both liable to make a mayonnaise curdle.

2. Make sure that there are no gelatinous threads left on the egg yolks. Put yolks in a medium-sized bowl and set it in a pan or on a damp cloth on the table to hold it steady. Add mustard and a pinch each of salt and freshly ground black pepper, and work to a smooth paste with a spoon or a whisk.

3. Add a teaspoon of lemon juice and work until smooth again.

4. Pour olive oil into a measuring jug. With a teaspoon, start adding oil to egg yolk mixture a drop at a time, beating well between each addition.

5. Having incorporated about a quarter of the oil, step up the rate at which you add the remainder

of the oil, a teaspoon or two at a time, or a steady, fine trickle, beating strongly as you do so. If the mayonnaise becomes very thick before all the oil has been absorbed, thin it down again with more lemon juice or a few drops of cold water. Forcing olive oil into a very thick mayonnaise is another factor which may cause it to curdle. The finished mayonnaise should be thick and shiny, and drop from the spoon or whisk in heavy globs.

6. Correct seasoning, adding more salt, freshly ground black pepper or lemon juice if necessary.

7. If mayonnaise is not to be used immediately, beat in a tablespoon of boiling water to keep it from separating. Cover bowl tightly and leave at the bottom of the refrigerator until ready to use.

Carciofi alla Romana

6 small artichokes
lemon juice
3 level tablespoons finely chopped parsley
3 cloves garlic, mashed
3 level tablespoons finely chopped fresh mint
2-4 anchovy fillets, mashed
6 level tablespoons fresh breadcrumbs
salt and freshly ground black pepper
150 ml/¼ pint olive oil
300 ml/½ pint dry white wine

1. Trim rough outer leaves and stems of artichokes. Wash the artichokes in cold water. Open leaves by pressing artichokes against corner of kitchen table. Spread leaves, cut out 'chokes' (fuzzy centres) and discard them. Sprinkle with lemon juice to prevent exposed hearts turning black.

2. Mix parsley, garlic, mint, anchovies, breadcrumbs, and salt and freshly ground black pepper, to taste, with a little of the olive oil and wine. Stuff artichokes with this mixture and place them, heads down, in a shallow casserole just large enough to hold them. Pour over remaining oil and wine and cover with oiled paper. Bake in a moderately hot oven (190°C, 375°F, Gas Mark 5) for about 45 minutes, or until tender. Serve cold in their own juices as an *hors-d'oeuvre*, or hot as a vegetable, Roman style.

Herb-stuffed Mushrooms *Serves 4 to 6*
Mushrooms à la Grecque *Serves 4 to 6*
Spinach-stuffed Tomatoes *Serves 4*

32

Herb-stuffed Mushrooms

16–24 open mushrooms, according to size
4 shallots, finely chopped
1 clove garlic, finely chopped
225 g/8 oz sausagemeat
2 level tablespoons finely chopped chervil
  or parsley
2 level tablespoons finely chopped tarragon
¼ level teaspoon dried thyme
2 bay leaves, crumbled
salt and freshly ground black pepper
olive oil
dried breadcrumbs
2–4 level tablespoons finely chopped parsley

1. Wipe mushrooms clean with a damp cloth and trim stem ends. Remove stems carefully from caps and chop them finely. Mix thoroughly with shallots, garlic, sausagemeat and herbs, and season to taste with salt and freshly ground black pepper.

2. Sauté mixture in 2 tablespoons olive oil until golden.

3. Brush insides of mushroom caps with olive oil. Fill with sausage mixture and sprinkle lightly with breadcrumbs and finely chopped parsley.

4. Pour 6 tablespoons olive oil into an ovenproof *gratin* dish and heat through in the oven. Place stuffed mushroom caps in the hot oil and cook in a moderately hot oven (190°C, 375°F, Gas Mark 5) for 15 to 20 minutes.

Mushrooms à la Grecque

450 g/1 lb thickly sliced mushrooms
1 (142-g/5-oz) can tomato purée
2–3 tablespoons olive oil or butter
½ Spanish onion, finely chopped
½ clove garlic, finely chopped
salt and freshly ground black pepper

Serve hot as a vegetable, cold as an appetiser.

1. Combine 1 can tomato purée and 2 cans water in a saucepan with olive oil or butter, finely chopped onion and garlic, and salt and freshly

ground black pepper to taste. Mix well, cover pan and bring to the boil. Simmer gently over the lowest of heats, stirring from time to time, for about 30 minutes, adding a little more water if necessary.

2. Add sliced mushrooms to sauce and simmer for 10 minutes.

Spinach-stuffed Tomatoes

8 large tomatoes
16 level tablespoons hot cooked spinach
butter
salt and freshly ground black pepper
4 level tablespoons freshly grated Parmesan
  cheese

1. Slice tops off tomatoes; scoop out interiors carefully and discard.

2. Cook spinach, drain well and while hot rub twice through a fine sieve. Add butter, and season to taste with salt and freshly ground black pepper.

3. Fill tomatoes with the hot purée, sprinkle with freshly grated Parmesan and dot with butter. Arrange filled tomatoes in a buttered baking dish and bake in a moderate oven (180°C, 350°F, Gas Mark 4) for 5 minutes.

Moroccan Carrot Appetiser

1 kg/2 lb carrots, peeled and cut in quarters
   lengthwise
6 tablespoons water
6 tablespoons olive oil
2 cloves garlic
salt and freshly ground black pepper
1–2 tablespoons vinegar
$\frac{1}{4}$ level teaspoon cayenne
$\frac{1}{4}$ level teaspoon paprika
$\frac{1}{2}$ level teaspoon powdered cumin
1–2 tablespoons finely chopped parsley

1. Blanch peeled quartered carrots in water to cover until water boils. Drain.

2. Simmer carrots until tender in water and olive oil, with garlic, and salt and freshly ground black pepper, to taste.

3. Drain, add vinegar, and generous amounts of salt and freshly ground black pepper. Flavour to taste with cayenne, paprika and powdered cumin. Garnish with finely chopped parsley. Serve cold as an appetiser.

Tian à la Provençale

4 small aubergines
4 small courgettes
olive oil
2 green peppers
2 red peppers
2 yellow peppers
4 cloves garlic, finely chopped
4–6 level tablespoons finely chopped parsley
thyme and marjoram
8 tomatoes
·butter
4–6 level tablespoons fresh breadcrumbs

1. Cut aubergines and courgettes in thin strips, and sauté separately in olive oil.

2. Cut peppers (green, red and yellow) in rings, and sauté in olive oil. A few minutes before the end of cooking, sprinkle the aubergines and courgettes with half the finely chopped garlic and half the parsley, and add thyme and marjoram, to taste.

3. Cut tomatoes into thick rounds. Place them in a buttered *gratin* dish and cook *à la provençale* with remaining garlic and parsley, and the breadcrumbs.

4. Arrange cooked vegetables in a large ovenproof *gratin* dish, with the tomatoes in the centre, the aubergines on one side, and the courgettes on the other. Then place red, yellow and green pepper rings in a lattice over vegetables. Brown under the grill and serve immediately. Also good served cold.

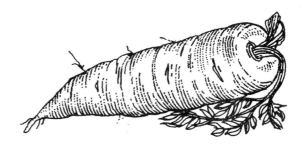

Italian Pepper Appetiser

4–6 green and red peppers
6 tomatoes, peeled and diced
2 cloves garlic, finely chopped
1 (56-g/2-oz) can anchovy fillets, drained
   and finely chopped
4 tablespoons dried breadcrumbs
olive oil
salt and freshly ground black pepper
2 tablespoons butter

1. Cut peppers in half lengthwise and scoop out seeds and fibres.

2. Combine diced tomatoes, finely chopped garlic and anchovies, breadcrumbs and 4 to 6 tablespoons olive oil. Season with salt and freshly ground black pepper.

3. Stuff pepper halves with this mixture and arrange them in a well-oiled ovenproof baking dish. Dot with butter and bake in a moderate oven (180°C, 350°F, Gas Mark 4) for 45 to 50 minutes, until tender. Serve cold.

34

Grilled Peppers en Salade

4–6 green, red or yellow peppers
well-flavoured French Dressing (see Seafood
   Salad, page 14)
lettuce leaves
1 (56-g/2-oz) can anchovy fillets
finely chopped garlic
finely chopped parsley

1. Grill or roast peppers as close to the heat as possible, turning them until the skin is charred on all sides. Rub off skins under running cold water. Core, seed and slice peppers into thick strips and marinate in a well-flavoured French Dressing.

2. Serve as an appetiser salad on a bed of lettuce leaves with a lattice of anchovy fillets and a sprinkle of finely chopped garlic and parsley for garnish. Or serve in an *hors-d'oeuvre* dish with French Dressing only.

Note: Peppers prepared in this way will keep a long time under refrigeration if packed in oil in sterilised airtight jars.

Polynesian Pork Saté

1 kg/2 lb lean pork
6 Brazil nuts, grated
1 level tablespoon ground coriander seed
2 cloves garlic, finely chopped
1 level tablespoon salt
1 Spanish onion, grated
4 tablespoons lemon juice
1–2 level tablespoons brown sugar
4 tablespoons soy sauce
1 level teaspoon crushed black pepper (or
   freshly ground black pepper, to taste)
$\frac{1}{8}$ level teaspoon crushed hot red pepper

1. Cut pork into 2.5-cm/1-inch cubes. Combine remaining ingredients in a large mixing bowl. Add pork cubes and allow them to marinate in this mixture for at least 2 hours.

2. **When ready to serve:** thread pork on metal skewers and grill over charcoal or under a gas or electric grill until cooked through.

Javanese Steak Satés

675 g/1$\frac{1}{2}$ lb rump steak, 2.5 cm/1 inch thick
2 tablespoons soy sauce
6 tablespoons olive oil
2 tablespoons lemon juice
$\frac{1}{4}$ Spanish onion, finely chopped
1 clove garlic, finely chopped
1 level tablespoon powdered cumin
freshly ground black pepper

1. Cut steak into thin strips 7.5 cm/3 inches long, and marinate for at·least 4 hours in a mixture of soy sauce, olive oil, lemon juice, finely chopped onion and garlic, and powdered cumin.

2. Thread the beef on skewers and brush with marinade. Grill over charcoal or under a gas or electric grill until done, turning the skewers from time to time. Season to taste with freshly ground black pepper.

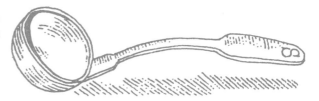

Pearl Buck's Sweet and Sour Spare Ribs

1.25 kg/2$\frac{1}{2}$ lb spare ribs of pork
450 ml/$\frac{3}{4}$ pint water
4 tablespoons soy sauce
salt
3 level tablespoons sugar or honey
3 tablespoons vinegar
1 level tablespoon cornflour
150 ml/$\frac{1}{4}$ pint water
2 tablespoons sake, or dry sherry and water
1 level teaspoon grated fresh ginger root

1. Cut ribs into separate pieces and cook in water with soy sauce and salt, to taste. Bring to the boil, turn down heat and allow to simmer for 1 hour.

2. Transfer to a frying pan, add remaining ingredients and fry until the gravy becomes translucent.

Marinated Smoked Salmon with Dill

225 g/8 oz sliced smoked salmon
1 level teaspoon whole black peppercorns
½ level teaspoon dill seed
1 bay leaf
300 ml/½ pint dry white wine
150 ml/¼ pint soured cream
2 level tablespoons prepared mustard
salt
lemon juice
1 tablespoon chopped chives
1 dill pickle, thinly sliced

1. Place salmon in a covered glass dish. Sprinkle with whole peppers and dill seed. Add bay leaf and cover with dry white wine. Place in refrigerator and allow salmon to marinate in this mixture overnight.

2. Just before serving, drain wine and spices from salmon. Place spices and half of the wine in a mixing bowl. Add soured cream and prepared mustard, and flavour to taste with salt and lemon juice.

3. Place salmon on a serving dish; cover with sauce and garnish with chopped chives and sliced pickle.

Soused Herrings

12 fresh herrings
1 Spanish onion, finely chopped
150 ml/¼ pint double cream
salt and freshly ground black pepper
2–3 level tablespoons pickling spice
dry cider or dry white wine
150 ml/¼ pint soured cream
½ cucumber, thinly sliced

1. Split herrings down the back; remove backbones carefully and stuff with their soft roes mixed with half the finely chopped onion, double cream, and salt and freshly ground black pepper, to taste.

2. Sprinkle half remaining chopped onion on the bottom of a shallow ovenproof baking dish, season with 1 tablespoon pickling spice and arrange the fish on this bed, head to tail.

3. Cover with remaining spice and finely chopped onion. Pour in dry cider or dry white wine to cover and bake in a moderately hot oven (190°C, 375°F, Gas Mark 5), covered, until fish flakes easily with a fork. Cool, then remove fish. Strain cooking liquids and blend with soured cream. Season to taste with salt and freshly ground black pepper. Arrange fish on a serving dish; pour over cream sauce and garnish with thinly sliced cucumber.

George's Insalata 'La Morra'

225 g/8 oz raw potatoes
white wine vinegar
225 g/8 oz cooked breast of chicken
1 slice cooked ham, 5 mm/¼ inch thick
1 slice cooked tongue, 5 mm/¼ inch thick
50 g/2 oz Fontina, Caerphilly or Double
 Gloucester cheese
150 ml/¼ pint well-flavoured mayonnaise
 (see page 89)
6–8 level tablespoons whipped cream
salt and freshly ground black pepper
canned white truffles

1. Cut raw potatoes into matchsticks and boil them for 15 to 20 minutes in a mixture of water and white wine vinegar, three-fifths vinegar to two-fifths water. Drain and chill.

2. Cut chicken, ham, tongue and cheese into matchsticks. Combine with potatoes and dress with mayonnaise and whipped cream seasoned to taste with salt and freshly ground black pepper.

3. Just before serving, grate truffles over top of salad.

Note: Fontina cheese is firm, not crumbly, and slightly piquant without being strongly flavoured. Caerphilly or Double Gloucester are probably the nearest English equivalents.

36

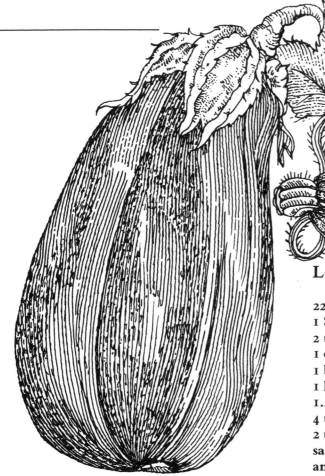

Lentil Salad

225 g/8 oz lentils
1 Spanish onion, finely chopped
2 tablespoons olive oil
1 clove garlic
1 bay leaf
1 level teaspoon salt
1.4 litres/2½ pints water
4 tablespoons olive oil
2 tablespoons wine vinegar
salt and freshly ground black pepper
anchovy fillets
tomato wedges
black olives

DRESSING
½ Spanish onion, finely chopped
6 level tablespoons finely chopped parsley
1 level teaspoon prepared mustard
salt and freshly ground black pepper
olive oil
juice of ½ lemon

1. Soak lentils overnight in water to cover. Drain.

2. Sauté finely chopped onion in olive oil until transparent. Add garlic, bay leaf, salt and water, and simmer lentils in this stock for about 2 hours, or until tender. Drain and cool; then add olive oil and wine vinegar, and season to taste with salt and freshly ground black pepper.

3. **To make dressing:** combine finely chopped onion, parsley, mustard, salt and freshly ground black pepper in a bowl. Mix well and then pour in

Courgette Appetiser

4 level tablespoons finely chopped onion
4 level tablespoons finely chopped carrot
4 level tablespoons butter
150 ml/¼ pint dry white wine
150 ml/¼ pint water
2 garlic cloves, crushed
1 bouquet garni (2 sprigs parsley, 1 sprig thyme, 1 bay leaf)
12 courgettes, sliced and unpeeled

1. Combine finely chopped onion, carrot and butter in a saucepan with dry white wine and water. Add crushed garlic cloves and *bouquet garni*, and simmer for 15 minutes. Add sliced unpeeled courgettes, and simmer until tender.

2. Transfer courgettes to an earthenware dish. Pour *court-bouillon* over, chill and serve.

Aubergines au Gratin *Serves 4 to 6*
Potato Salad Niçoise *Serves 4 to 6*
Salade de Boeuf *Serves 4 to 6*

olive oil little by little, beating the mixture continuously, until sauce thickens. Flavour to taste with lemon juice.

4. Pour dressing over lentils and mix thoroughly. Garnish with anchovy fillets, tomato wedges and black olives.

Aubergines au Gratin

4 aubergines
salt
4 tablespoons olive oil
butter
1 Spanish onion, finely chopped
3 level tablespoons tomato purée
6 tomatoes, peeled, seeded and coarsely
   chopped
1-2 cloves garlic, finely chopped
3 level tablespoons finely chopped
   parsley
freshly ground black pepper
generous pinch each of allspice,
   cinnamon and sugar
dried breadcrumbs

1. Peel and dice aubergines, salt them liberally and leave to drain in a colander for 1 hour. Rinse off salt with cold water and shake diced aubergines dry in a cloth.

2. Combine olive oil and 2 tablespoons butter in a frying pan, and sauté aubergines until golden.

3. Remove from pan, and in the same oil fry onion until soft and just turning golden, adding more oil if necessary.

4. Add tomato purée, chopped tomatoes, and finely chopped garlic and parsley, and season to taste with salt, pepper, allspice, cinnamon and sugar. Simmer mixture, stirring occasionally, for 5 minutes.

5. Add diced aubergines to the mixture and pour into a buttered *gratin* dish (or individual soufflé dishes). Sprinkle with breadcrumbs, dot with butter and bake in a moderately hot oven (190°C, 375°F, Gas Mark 5) for 30 minutes.

This Turkish dish makes an excellent *hors-d'oeuvre*, served hot or cold.

Potato Salad Niçoise

1 kg/2 lb long thin salad potatoes
6-8 tablespoons olive oil
6-8 tablespoons dry white wine or beef
   consommé
2-3 tablespoons wine vinegar
6 level tablespoons finely chopped shallots
3 level tablespoons finely chopped parsley
salt and freshly ground black pepper
anchovy fillets
black olives
tomatoes

1. Boil long thin salad potatoes in their skins until cooked through. Peel and cut into thick slices. While still hot, pour over marinade of olive oil, dry white wine (or beef consommé) and wine vinegar. Add finely chopped shallots and parsley. Season to taste with salt and freshly ground black pepper.

2. Arrange anchovies in a latticework on top and place a black olive in the centre of each square. Garnish salad with a ring of tomato slices.

Salade de Boeuf

675 g/1½ lb boiled beef
6 gherkins, thinly sliced
6 level tablespoons finely chopped onion
6-8 tablespoons olive oil
2-3 tablespoons wine vinegar
salt and freshly ground black pepper
2 level tablespoons coarsely chopped
   gherkins
2 level tablespoons finely chopped parsley

Trim fat from beef and cut in small, thin slices. Mix with thinly sliced gherkins and finely chopped onion, and dress with olive oil, wine vinegar, and salt and freshly ground black pepper, to taste. Toss well and marinate in this mixture for at least 2 hours before serving. Garnish with chopped gherkins and parsley.

Hot and Cold Toasts and Canapés

38

Smoked Trout Canapés

4 smoked trout
double cream
olive oil
lemon juice
salt and freshly ground black pepper
sliced white bread
softened butter
finely chopped radishes
finely chopped parsley

1. Remove skin and bones from smoked trout and pound fillets to a paste in a mortar with 2 table-spoons each double cream and olive oil. Transfer mixture to an electric blender and add more cream and olive oil in equal quantities until mixture is of a spreadable consistency. Season to taste with lemon juice, salt and freshly ground black pepper. Chill.

2. Toast white bread and cut rounds of toast with a glass or biscuit cutter. Spread each round with softened butter and then cover generously with smoked trout mixture. Sprinkle with finely chopped radishes and parsley.

La Croûte Landaise

225 g/8 oz button mushrooms, sliced
6 level tablespoons butter
6 level tablespoons double cream
salt and freshly ground black pepper
4 fat slices brioche
4 thin rounds mousse de foie gras
1 egg yolk
150 ml/¼ pint Cream Sauce (see Omelette Bénédictine, page 24)
2 tablespoons freshly grated Parmesan cheese

1. Simmer sliced mushrooms in butter until soft. Purée them with cream; season to taste with salt and freshly ground black pepper.

2. Toast *brioche* slices. Spread each slice thickly with mushroom purée and place on a baking sheet. Top each 'toast' with a slice of *foie gras*. Add egg yolk to hot Cream Sauce and spoon over each 'toast'. Cover with freshly grated Parmesan and grill until golden.

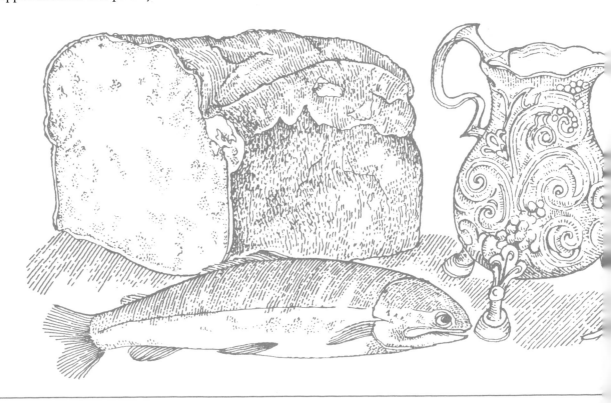

39

Swiss Bacon and Mushroom Toasts

12 thin slices white bread
225 g/8 oz Swiss cheese, grated
150 ml/¼ pint double cream
4 eggs
150 ml/¼ pint milk
8 level tablespoons butter

FILLING
12 rashers bacon
12–14 mushrooms, finely sliced
2 tablespoons butter
2 tablespoons lemon juice

1. To make filling for 6 sandwiches: fry bacon over moderate heat. Drain on kitchen paper. Sauté finely sliced mushrooms in butter and lemon juice. Use about 1 tablespoon mushrooms and 2 rashers trimmed bacon to fill each sandwich.

2. Trim crusts from bread. Mix Swiss cheese and cream and spread on all bread slices. Add a filling to half the bread slices; top with remaining slices, cheese side down. Beat eggs and milk with a fork. Dip sandwiches into egg mixture, coating both sides.

3. Heat butter until bubbling in a large frying pan; brown sandwiches on both sides over moderate heat. Serve with knife and fork or cut into bite-sized pieces.

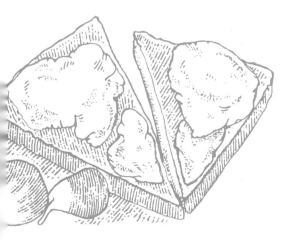

L'Anchoïade – Hot Anchovy Canapés

1 (56-g/2-oz) can anchovy fillets in oil
1 large clove garlic, crushed
1 tablespoon olive oil
2 level tablespoons softened butter
few drops lemon juice or cognac
freshly ground black pepper
4–6 thick slices white bread

1. Combine anchovy fillets, crushed garlic, olive oil and softened butter in a mortar, and pound to a smooth paste. Season to taste with a few drops of lemon juice or cognac and a little freshly ground black pepper.

2. Slice bread in half; toast on one side only and, while still hot, spread *anchoïade* paste on untoasted side, pressing paste well into bread. Toast in a hot oven for a few minutes just before serving.

Brioches Farcies

8 tiny brioches or 4 normal-sized ones
2 smoked sausages, finely chopped
50 g/2 oz ham, finely chopped
4 tablespoons milk
4 tablespoons cream
6–8 level tablespoons freshly grated Gruyère
   cheese
freshly ground black pepper
salt
1 tablespoon cognac

1. Cut caps off *brioches* and empty them. Pick apart interiors and combine with finely chopped meat of smoked sausages and ham. Add milk, cream and grated Gruyère and cook over a very low heat, stirring all the while, until you get a very thick paste. Add pepper, and a very little salt (sausages and ham are already rather salty). All this can be prepared in advance.

2. When ready to serve: reheat the mixture, stirring constantly. When it is very hot, remove from heat and stir in cognac; fill *brioches* with this mixture, replace caps and heat in the oven for a few minutes until warmed through.

Pancakes and Fritters

40

Basic French Crêpes (for Savoury Fillings)

6 tablespoons plain flour
½ level teaspoon salt
2 eggs
450 ml/¾ pint milk
butter or oil
2 tablespoons cognac (optional)

1. Sift flour and salt into a mixing bowl. Beat eggs and add them to dry ingredients. Mix in the milk and 2 tablespoons melted butter or oil gradually to avoid lumps. Add cognac if desired. Strain batter through a fine sieve and let it stand for at least 2 hours before cooking. Batter should be as thin as cream. Add a little water if too thick.

2. For each *crêpe*, spoon about 2 tablespoons batter into buttered pan, swirling pan to allow to cover entire surface thinly. Brush a piece of butter around edge of hot pan with the point of a knife. Cook over a medium heat until just golden but not brown – about 1 minute each side. Repeat until all *crêpes* are cooked, stacking them on a plate as they are ready.

Italian Ham and Cheese Pancakes

½ recipe Basic French Crêpes (see above)
225 g/8 oz Mozzarella cheese
4 thin slices prosciutto (raw Parma ham)
butter
4 level tablespoons plain flour
300 ml/½ pint hot milk
salt
cayenne
½ level teaspoon ground nutmeg
300 ml/½ pint double cream
2 egg yolks, well beaten
150 ml/¼ pint well-flavoured Italian Tomato Sauce (see Polenta Pasticciata, page 59)

1. Make 8 to 12 *crêpes* before making ham and cheese filling.

2. Cut 8 to 12 thin slices Mozzarella cheese and put aside for later use. Dice the remaining cheese and the ham.

3. Melt 2 tablespoons butter in the top of a double saucepan. Stir in flour and cook over water, stirring constantly, until smooth. Add hot milk and continue to cook, stirring constantly, until thickened. Season to taste with salt, cayenne and nutmeg.

4. Combine cream and beaten egg yolks in a bowl. Pour in some of the hot sauce and whisk until smooth. Return cream and egg mixture to the saucepan, add diced cheese and ham, and cook over water until sauce is smooth, thick and golden. Do not let sauce boil after eggs are added or it will curdle. Let mixture cool.

5. Spread a thin coating of well-flavoured Italian Tomato Sauce over each pancake and then cover generously with cheese and ham filling. Roll pancakes and put them in a well-buttered rectangular baking dish. Chill until 1 hour before using.

6. When nearing time to serve, spoon a little Tomato Sauce over each pancake and top with a thin strip of Mozzarella cheese. Bake for 20 minutes in a moderate oven (180°C, 350°F, Gas Mark 4).

Italian Spinach Pancakes

½ recipe Basic French Crêpes (see above)
350 g/12 oz frozen spinach
butter
salt and freshly ground black pepper
225 g/8 oz Ricotta or cottage cheese
3 eggs, lightly beaten
freshly grated Parmesan cheese
150 ml/¼ pint double cream
freshly grated nutmeg
300 ml/½ pint well-flavoured Italian Tomato Sauce (see Polenta Pasticciata, page 59)

1. Make 8 to 12 *crêpes* before making the spinach and cheese filling.

2. Cook spinach with 2 tablespoons butter, and season to taste with salt and freshly ground black pepper. Drain thoroughly, and add Ricotta or cottage cheese, the beaten eggs, 25-50 g/1-2 oz grated Parmesan, cream and nutmeg, to taste.

3. Spread each pancake generously with spinach and cheese filling. Roll pancakes and put them in a well-buttered rectangular baking dish. Chill until 1 hour before using.

4. When nearing time to serve, brush each pancake with melted butter and sprinkle with freshly grated Parmesan. Bake for 20 minutes in a moderate oven (180°C, 350°F, Gas Mark 4). Serve with well-flavoured Italian Tomato Sauce.

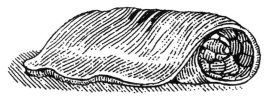

Crêpes aux Fruits de Mer

½ recipe Basic French Crêpes (see page 40)
1–2 level tablespoons each freshly grated
   Gruyère and Parmesan cheese

SEAFOOD FILLING
3 level tablespoons finely chopped onion
3 level tablespoons finely chopped shallots
3 level tablespoons butter
3 level tablespoons finely chopped raw veal
   or cooked ham
3 level tablespoons plain flour
salt and freshly ground black pepper
¼ level teaspoon nutmeg and cayenne mixed
1 bay leaf, crumbled
3 level tablespoons chopped parsley
600 ml/1 pint warm milk
2 egg yolks, well beaten
4 level tablespoons double cream
2 tablespoons lemon juice
4–6 tablespoons dry white wine
3 level tablespoons freshly grated Parmesan
   cheese
450 g/1 lb diced freshly cooked lobster, crab
   or mussels, or a combination of the three

1. Make *crêpes* and cover them with waxed paper or foil to prevent them drying out.

2. **To make seafood filling:** sauté finely chopped onion and shallots in butter until transparent. Add finely chopped veal or ham and continue to cook, stirring constantly, for 2 to 3 minutes.

Sprinkle with flour and cook, stirring, for 2 minutes more. Season to taste with salt, freshly ground black pepper, nutmeg and cayenne pepper. Add crumbled bay leaf, chopped parsley and half the warm milk, and stir until well blended.

3. Transfer contents to the top of a double saucepan. Add remaining milk and cook over water for 1 hour, stirring from time to time. Strain into a bowl in which you have whisked egg yolks, double cream, lemon juice and white wine. Return to heat and cook until thickened. (Do not allow sauce to boil or eggs will curdle.) Stir in grated cheese and diced shellfish, and heat through.

4. **To serve:** top each *crêpe* with 2 tablespoons prepared filling, and roll loosely. Place in rows in a rectangular baking dish. Top with remaining sauce and 1 or 2 tablespoons each freshly grated Gruyère and Parmesan cheese. Place under a preheated grill and cook until golden brown.

Mushroom Fritters

100 g/4 oz plain flour
¼ level teaspoon salt
2 egg yolks
1 tablespoon melted butter
150 ml/¼ pint white wine, cider or ale
150 ml/¼ pint milk or water
2 egg whites, stiffly beaten
225 g/8 oz button mushrooms
juice of 1 lemon
salt and freshly ground black pepper
oil for frying

1. Sift flour and salt together, make a well in the centre, and into this pour the egg yolks and cool melted butter. Stir briskly, drawing the flour in by degrees and adding white wine, cider or ale, a little at a time. Let it stand for 1 hour.

2. When ready to cook, stir in milk or water and fold in the stiffly beaten egg whites.

3. Wash mushrooms and sprinkle with lemon juice and seasoning. Dip each mushroom in the batter and fry in hot oil until golden. Drain well and serve very hot.

42 | Russian Blini

600 ml/1 pint milk
1 level tablespoon yeast
225 g/8 oz buckwheat flour (or half
buckwheat and half plain flour)
½ level teaspoon salt
3 egg yolks
melted butter
1 level tablespoon sugar
3 egg whites, stiffly beaten
soured cream
caviar and lemon wedges (optional)

1. Heat half the milk until lukewarm and combine in a warm bowl with yeast. Sift flour together with salt, and add enough of this to the liquid to make a thick 'sponge'. Cover bowl. Stand in a warm place and let sponge rise for about 2½ hours.

2. Beat egg yolks and whisk into remaining milk. Add 2 tablespoons melted butter and the sugar, and add to raised sponge mixture with remaining sifted flour. Beat well and let stand, covered, for 30 minutes more.

3. When ready to serve, fold in stiffly beaten egg whites. Cook on a buttered griddle (I use an iron Swedish *plattar* pan with indentations. *Blini* should be about 7.5 cm/3 inches in diameter.

4. Serve *blini* hot with melted butter and soured cream, or for special occasions, with soured cream, caviar and lemon wedges.

Hard-boiled Egg Fritters

4 hard-boiled eggs
1 slice bacon, 5 mm/¼ inch thick
½ Spanish onion, finely chopped
4 level tablespoons butter
4 level tablespoons finely chopped parsley
450 ml/¾ pint cold well-flavoured Béchamel
Sauce (see page 84)
salt and freshly ground black pepper
1 egg, beaten
dried breadcrumbs
oil or fat for frying
lemon wedges

1. Shell and chop eggs coarsely.

2. Chop bacon and sauté with finely chopped onion in butter until onion begins to colour.

3. Combine chopped eggs, bacon, onion and finely chopped parsley. Mix well and then stir into cold Béchamel Sauce. Season to taste with salt and freshly ground black pepper. Form mixture loosely into balls and chill.

4. When ready to cook, remove from refrigerator and re-form into more perfect shapes – patties, balls or cork shapes. Dip in beaten egg and then in breadcrumbs. Fry in hot oil until golden. Drain well and serve very hot with lemon wedges.

Crêpes 'Alfredo'

Illustrated on page 45

FILLING
1.75–2.25 kg/4–5 lb fresh spinach
butter
350 g/12 oz raw chicken (breast or legs)
2 small onions
½ clove garlic
150 ml/¼ pint double cream
salt and freshly ground black pepper

CRÊPE BATTER
125 g/4½ oz plain flour
300 ml/½ pint milk
3 eggs
2 level tablespoons melted butter

CHEESE SAUCE
100 g/4 oz butter
100 g/4 oz plain flour
1.15 litres/2 pints milk
350 g/12 oz Parmesan cheese, freshly grated
salt and freshly ground black pepper

1. Wash spinach well, removing any yellowed or damaged leaves. Drain and then remove stalks. Sauté spinach leaves in a pan with 4 level tablespoons butter, stirring constantly, until spinach 'melts'. Transfer to a large sieve and press out excess liquid.

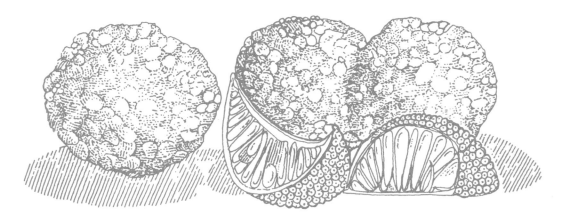

2. Remove skin from chicken, and cut meat into thin strips.

3. Chop onions and garlic finely and sauté in 2 level tablespoons butter over a low heat, stirring from time to time, until onions are transparent. Add chicken meat and continue to cook, stirring, until chicken is tender. Remove from heat.

4. Combine spinach and chicken and onion mixture and pass through the fine blade of a mincer. Add double cream and salt and freshly ground black pepper, to taste.

5. To make batter: combine flour, milk, eggs and melted butter in an electric blender and blend well. Pour batter into a bowl and leave to rest for at least 30 minutes before making crêpes.

6. To make savoury pancakes for Crêpes Alfredo: when ready to fry crêpes, cover an upturned soup plate with a folded cloth. Heat a small, heavy crêpe pan about 15 cm/6 inches in diameter. When it is very hot, rub entire surface very lightly with a wad of kitchen paper moistened with oil. Pour about 2 tablespoons batter into centre of hot pan, tilting it quickly so that it coats bottom of pan very thinly and evenly all over before it has had a chance to set. If you find you have used too much batter, pour excess back into the bowl once a thin layer has set on the bottom of the pan, and scrape away the 'trail' it leaves on the side of the pan. Then use a little less batter for the next crêpe. Cook steadily for 1

minute, drawing a spatula or the point of a knife round edges of crêpe to loosen it. As soon as small bubbles begin to form under the crêpe, flip it over and cook for 60 to 90 seconds longer. Slip out on the prepared plate and cover with the cloth. Continue in this manner until you have made 12 crêpes in all, with an extra one or two as a reserve, stacking them on top of each other under the cloth. Oil pan lightly between each crêpe.

7. To make sauce: melt butter in the top of a double saucepan. Stir in flour and cook over a low heat, stirring constantly until a pale *roux* is formed – about 2 minutes. Bring milk to the boil in a saucepan and add milk gradually to *roux*, stirring constantly so that no lumps form. Cook over lightly simmering water for 20 minutes. Then add freshly grated Parmesan, reserving 6 level tablespoons for later use. Season with salt and freshly ground black pepper to taste. Keep sauce warm.

8. To assemble crêpes: butter a large rectangular flameproof baking dish generously. Place 12 crêpes out on your working surface. Fill each crêpe generously with a few tablespoons of the spinach filling and roll up. Gently place crêpes side by side in the baking dish and put in a very cool to cool oven (120°C to 140°C, 250°F to 275°F, Gas Mark ½ to 1).

9. Remove crêpes from oven; pour sauce over crêpes and sprinkle with remaining grated Parmesan. Place under grill for a few more minutes, or until sauce is bubbling. Serve immediately.

Soufflés

44

Easy Salmon Soufflé

4 tablespoons butter
3 tablespoons flour
300 ml/½ pint milk
8 tablespoons grated Parmesan cheese
1 (212-g/7½-oz) can salmon
little cream
salt
cayenne
4 egg yolks
5 egg whites

1. Melt butter in the top of a double saucepan. Add flour and stir until well blended. Add milk and continue cooking, stirring continuously, until the sauce has thickened. Stir in grated cheese and heat until cheese has melted into the mixture. Add canned salmon, pounded to a smooth paste with a little cream to make soufflé smooth. Heat through. Season generously with salt and cayenne.

2. Beat egg yolks in a bowl and pour hot salmon mixture over them, stirring until well blended.

3. Beat egg whites until stiff and gently fold them into mixture, a little at a time. Pour in a buttered and floured 20-cm/8-inch soufflé dish and set in a pan of hot water. Bake in a preheated moderate oven (180°C, 350°F, Gas Mark 4) for 25 to 30 minutes. Serve at once.

Mussel Soufflé

24 mussels
300 ml/½ pint dry white wine
3 level tablespoons finely chopped parsley
2 sprigs thyme
1 bay leaf
freshly ground black pepper
2 level tablespoons butter
2 level tablespoons flour
300 ml/½ pint hot milk
4 level tablespoons grated Parmesan cheese
salt
4 tablespoons mussel liquor
4 eggs

1. **To prepare mussels:** place mussels in a bowl and wash well under running water. Scrape each shell with a knife, removing all traces of mud, seaweed and barnacles. Discard any mussels with cracked, broken or opened shells: **they are dangerous**. Rinse again in running water and remove 'beards'.

2. **To cook mussels:** combine dry white wine, finely chopped parsley, thyme, bay leaf and freshly ground black pepper in a saucepan. Add mussels, cover saucepan and steam mussels, shaking the pan constantly until shells open.

3. Shell mussels, reserving liquor, and chop coarsely.

4. Melt butter in a saucepan, add flour and stir until smooth. Add hot milk and stir over low heat until thick. Remove from heat. Add grated Parmesan and season to taste with salt and freshly ground black pepper. Stir in chopped mussels and mussel liquor, and allow the mixture to cool slightly.

5. Separate eggs. Beat yolks lightly and stir into sauce. Beat whites until they are stiff but not dry, and fold into sauce. Pour into a 20-cm/8-inch soufflé dish around which you have tied grease-proof paper to make a high 'collar'.

6. Bake soufflé in a preheated moderate oven (180°C, 350°F, Gas Mark 4) for 45 minutes. Serve immediately.

Crêpes 'Alfredo' (see page 42)

French Onion Tart (see page 54); **Spinach and Egg Tart** (see page 55); **Hot Mushroom Tart** (see page 55);
Courgette and Bacon Tart (see page 52); **Pizza Tart** (see page 53)

Provençal Tomato and Onion Tart (see page 54)

Creamed Button Onion Tart (see page 51)

French Mushroom Tartlets (see page 52)

Langouste Soufflé

2 live langoustes or lobsters (about 1 kg/2 lb
  each)
300 ml/½ pint Béchamel Sauce (see page 84)
fresh butter
paprika
salt and freshly ground black pepper
150 ml/¼ pint double cream
4 egg yolks
5 egg whites, stiffly beaten

1. Cook *langoustes* or lobsters in salted boiling
water for 25 minutes. Allow them to cool in their
own juices.

2. Cut shells in half and remove flesh. Pound
flesh in a mortar with 2 to 3 tablespoons each
thick Béchamel Sauce and butter. Season to taste
with paprika, salt and freshly ground black pepper.

3. Combine remaining Béchamel Sauce and
double cream in the top of a double saucepan. Add
pounded *langoustes* or lobsters and cook over
water, stirring constantly, until sauce is smooth
and thick.

4. Beat egg yolks in a bowl until well blended.
Stir in a little of the hot Béchamel Sauce and then
return egg mixture to remaining sauce. Cook over
water, stirring from time to time, until sauce is
thick. But do not allow sauce to boil, or it will
curdle. Remove from heat and beat until slightly
cooled. Then fold stiffly beaten egg whites into
the sauce; correct seasoning and fill empty
langouste shells with mixture.

5. Arrange buttered foil around shells to form a
'collar' so that mixture will not run over. Place
shells in a pan with a little hot water and cook in a
preheated moderate oven (180°C, 350°F, Gas
Mark 4) for about 20 minutes, or until soufflés are
puffed and golden.

Herring Soufflé

49

4 level tablespoons butter
2 level tablespoons flour
300 ml/½ pint milk
½ Spanish onion, finely chopped
2 level tablespoons finely chopped parsley
1 level tablespoon anchovy paste
salt
nutmeg
cayenne
175 g/6 oz cooked herring fillets, finely
  chopped
4 egg yolks, lightly beaten
5 egg whites

1. Melt 3 tablespoons butter in the top of a double
saucepan, add flour and stir until smooth. Add
milk and stir over low heat until thick. Remove
from heat.

2. Sauté finely chopped onion in remaining butter
until transparent. Combine with parsley and stir
into sauce. Add anchovy paste, and salt, nutmeg
and cayenne, to taste. Stir finely chopped cooked
herring fillets into soufflé mixture. Remove saucepan from heat and allow mixture to cool slightly.
Stir in lightly beaten egg yolks; blend well.

3. Beat whites until they are stiff but not dry, and
fold gently into sauce. Pour into a 20-cm/8-inch
soufflé dish around which you have tied grease-
proof paper to make a high 'collar'. Bake soufflé
in a preheated moderate oven (180°C, 350°F, Gas
Mark 4) for 45 minutes. Serve immediately.

Quiches

50

Quiche Lorraine

shortcrust pastry (see page 90)
4 eggs
150 ml/¼ pint double cream
150 ml/¼ pint milk
**150 ml/¼ pint well-flavoured stock (chicken,
    beef or veal)**
salt and freshly ground black pepper
freshly grated nutmeg
**100 g/4 oz green bacon, or fat salt pork,
    cut in 1 piece**
2 level tablespoons butter
100 g/4 oz Gruyère cheese, diced

1. Line pastry tin (or individual tins) with short-crust pastry. Prick bottom with a fork, brush with a little beaten egg and bake 'blind' for 15 minutes.

2. Whisk eggs in a bowl. Add cream, milk and stock and whisk until thick and lemon coloured. Flavour to taste with salt, freshly ground black pepper and freshly grated nutmeg.

3. Cut green bacon, or fat salt pork, into finger-shaped strips. Remove rind and blanch in boiling water for 3 minutes. Drain and sauté strips in butter until golden. Drain.

4. Arrange diced cheese and bacon or pork strips in bottom of pastry case. Pour over the cream and egg mixture and bake in a moderate oven (160°C, 325°F, Gas Mark 3) for 30 to 40 minutes, until the custard is set and golden brown. Serve hot.

Cassolette de Sole 'Mirabelle'

22 g/8 oz puff pastry (see page 90)
2 sole (450 g/1 lb each), filleted
2 shallots
butter
12 mussels
4 oysters, shelled
salt and freshly ground black pepper
1 glass dry white wine
300 ml/½ pint cream

1. Take 4 flan moulds 10 cm/4 inches across, roll the pastry out very thinly and line the moulds.

Bake 'blind' in a moderately hot oven (200°C, 400°F, Gas Mark 6) for 10 minutes, remove beans and return to a moderate oven (180°C, 350°F, Gas Mark 4) for 5 to 10 minutes.

2. Fold fillets over. Chop shallots finely, and put fish and shallots in a saucepan with a good-sized piece of butter, mussels, oysters, salt, freshly ground black pepper, wine and cream.

3. Allow to cook for 12 minutes, and then remove the fish and shellfish. Take the mussels out of their shells. Reduce the sauce until thick and add 2 tablespoons butter.

4. Warm the pastry cases in the oven for 2 minutes, fill with fish and shellfish, and pour the sauce over the top.

Artichoke Tarts Vinaigrette

4 cooked or canned artichoke hearts
4 hard-boiled eggs
1 thick slice cooked ham, diced
½ cucumber, peeled, seeded and diced
4 sticks celery, sliced
olive oil
wine vinegar
dry mustard
finely chopped garlic
salt and freshly ground black pepper
**6 individual shortcrust pastry cases, baked
    'blind' (see page 90)**
finely chopped fresh herbs
mayonnaise (see page 89)

1. Dice artichoke hearts and hard-boiled eggs into large pieces and combine in a bowl with diced cooked ham, cucumber and celery.

2. Moisten liberally with a well-flavoured vinaigrette dressing made from 3 parts olive oil, 1 part wine vinegar, dry mustard, finely chopped garlic, salt and freshly ground black pepper, to taste.

3. When ready to serve: fill baked pastry cases with artichoke and egg. Sprinkle each tart with finely chopped fresh herbs and top with a dab of stiff mayonnaise.

Creamed Button Onion Tart
Illustrated on page 47

**20-cm/8-inch shortcrust pastry case, baked
    'blind' (see page 90)**
melted butter (optional)

FILLING
675 g/2 lb tiny button onions
salt
300 ml/½ pint milk
1 bay leaf
3 black peppercorns
2 cloves
½ chicken stock cube
½ level teaspoon butter
½ level teaspoon flour
3 egg yolks
6 level tablespoons double cream
**2 level teaspoons freshly grated Parmesan
    cheese**
freshly ground black pepper
freshly grated nutmeg

1. To make filling: peel button onions. Put in a
pan with cold salted water to cover. Bring to the
boil over a moderate heat, boil for 2 minutes then
drain thoroughly in a colander.

2. In another pan, combine milk with bay leaf,
peppercorns, cloves and half a chicken stock cube.
Bring to the boil, remove from heat and leave to
infuse for 30 minutes, covered with a lid.

3. Add onions to infused milk and return to the
heat. Bring to the boil again and poach gently for
5 to 7 minutes, until onions have softened but
still hold their shape.

4. Place the prebaked tart case, still in its tin, on a
baking sheet.

5. When onions are tender, remove them from
the milk with a slotted spoon and arrange them
side by side in the pastry case. Strain remaining
milk through a fine sieve.

6. Melt butter in a heavy pan. Add flour and stir
over a low heat for a minute or two until well
blended to make a pale *roux*. Then gradually

blend in strained milk, stirring constantly to make
a smooth sauce, and simmer for a few minutes
longer until thickened.

7. In a large bowl, beat egg yolks lightly with
cream until well mixed. Gradually pour in a
ladleful of hot sauce, beating all the while. Then
pour all the sauce into the top of a double saucepan
and stir over hot water until it thickens, taking
great care not to let it come to the boil, or the egg
yolks will curdle. Finally, stir in freshly grated
Parmesan and season generously with salt, freshly
ground black pepper and freshly grated nutmeg.

8. Spoon sauce over onions in tart case and bake in
a moderate oven (180°C, 350°F, Gas Mark 4) for
30 minutes, or until filling has set and top is a rich
golden colour. If tart has not browned by the time
filling is firm, brush top lightly with melted butter
and slip under a hot grill for a minute or two to
colour it. Serve hot.

Smoked Salmon Quiche

4 eggs
150 ml/¼ pint double cream
150 ml/¼ pint milk
**150 ml/¼ pint canned clam juice or well-
    flavoured fish stock**
salt and freshly ground black pepper
grated nutmeg
**8 individual shortcrust pastry cases (about
    10 cm/4 inches in diameter)**
thinly sliced smoked salmon
butter

1. Whisk eggs together with cream, milk and
canned clam juice, or a well-flavoured fish stock.
When well mixed, season to taste with salt,
freshly ground black pepper and grated nutmeg.

2. Prick bottoms of pastry cases with a fork and
bake 'blind' in a hot oven (230°C, 450°F, Gas Mark
8) for about 15 minutes, just long enough to set
the crusts without browning them. Allow to cool.

3. Fill pastry cases with egg mixture. Cover with
thin slices of smoked salmon and dot with butter.
Bake in a moderate oven (160°C, 325°F, Gas Mark
3) for 30 to 40 minutes, and serve immediately.

52

Courgette and Bacon Tart
Illustrated on page 46

**23- or 25-cm/9- or 10-inch shortcrust pastry
case, baked 'blind' (see page 90)**

FILLING
**½ Spanish onion
2 tablespoons olive oil
100 g/4 oz green bacon, cut in 1 piece
4-6 small courgettes
salt and freshly ground black pepper
4 eggs
300 ml/½ pint cream
150 ml/¼ pint milk
freshly grated nutmeg
6 level tablespoons freshly grated Gruyère
cheese**

GARNISH
sprigs of fresh watercress (optional)

1. Chop onion finely and sauté in olive oil until
soft, stirring constantly so that it does not take on
colour. Remove onion from pan with a slotted
spoon and reserve.

2. Cut green bacon into 5-mm/¼-inch slices and
then cut each slice into 'fingers' about 5 mm/¼
inch thick. Sauté in oil until golden. Remove from
pan with slotted spoon and reserve.

3. Wash courgettes and cut off tops and bottoms.
Slice courgettes as thinly as you can and sauté
slices in remaining fats until lightly coloured.
Season to taste with salt and freshly ground black
pepper. Remove from pan with slotted spoon
and reserve.

4. Combine eggs, cream and milk in a mixing
bowl and mix thoroughly. Season generously
with salt, freshly ground black pepper and freshly
grated nutmeg.

5. Sprinkle 2 level tablespoons grated Gruyère on
the bottom of prepared pastry case. Combine
sautéed onion, bacon and courgettes and spoon
into pastry case. Sprinkle with 2 level tablespoons
grated Gruyère and pour in egg and cream
mixture.

6. Sprinkle with remaining Gruyère and bake in a
moderate oven (160°C, 325°F, Gas Mark 3) for
30 to 40 minutes until the custard is set and is
golden brown. Garnish if desired.

French Mushroom Tartlets
Illustrated on page 48

**4-6 baked shortcrust pastry cases (see
page 90)
450-675 g/1-1½ lb small button mushrooms
4 tablespoons butter
2 tablespoons olive oil
salt and freshly ground black pepper
pinch of cayenne
4-6 tablespoons Madeira
3 egg yolks
300 ml/½ pint double cream
finely chopped parsley**

1. Wash or wipe the mushrooms and trim rough
stem ends.

2. Sauté mushrooms in butter and olive oil for 3
minutes (the mushrooms should still be crisp).
Season generously with salt and freshly ground
black pepper, and a pinch of cayenne. Add
Madeira and toss well. Remove pan from heat.

3. Whisk the egg yolks lightly and beat into the
double cream. Cook the mixture in a double
saucepan, stirring constantly, until mixture
thickens. Be careful not to allow the cream to come
to the boil, or the sauce will curdle. Add to the
mushrooms in the pan and heat *gently*, stirring all
the time.

4. To serve: place the baked pastry cases on a
baking tray and fill each case with the mushroom
and Madeira mixture. Spoon over any remaining
Madeira sauce and place under the grill for a
minute or two to heat through. Sprinkle with
finely chopped parsley and serve immediately.

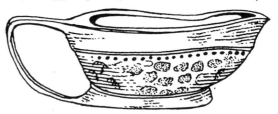

Prawn and Lobster Quiche

PASTRY
225 g/8 oz plain flour
1 level tablespoon icing sugar
generous pinch of salt
150 g/5 oz butter, diced and softened
1-2 tablespoons iced water

QUICHE FILLING
150 ml/¼ pint double cream
150 ml/¼ pint milk
150 ml/¼ pint canned clam juice
4 eggs
1 (198-g/7-oz) can lobster meat
100 g/4 oz prawns

1. To make pastry: sift flour, sugar and salt into
a mixing bowl. Rub in softened butter a little bit at
a time with the tips of the fingers until mixture
resembles fine breadcrumbs. Do this very gently
and lightly or mixture will become greasy and
heavy. Add just enough iced water to make a
good dough. Shape dough lightly into a flattened
round, wrap in foil or polythene and put in refrigerator for at least 1 hour to ripen and become firm.
If chilled dough is too firm for handling, leave at
room temperature until it softens slightly. Then
turn out on to a floured board and roll out in usual
manner. Place in a 23-cm/9-inch pie tin and press
out with fingertips. Prick with a fork, cover with
a piece of foil and fill with dried beans. Bake
'blind' in a hot oven (230°C, 450°F, Gas Mark 8)
for 15 minutes. Remove beans and foil. Allow
pastry case to cool.

2. To make quiche filling and to serve: beat
cream, milk, clam juice and eggs with a whisk.
Place chunks of lobster and prawns on the baked
pastry case. Pour the beaten egg mixture over the
lobster and prawns. Bake in a moderate oven
(160°C, 325°F, Gas Mark 3) for 30 to 40 minutes,
until the custard is set and golden brown.

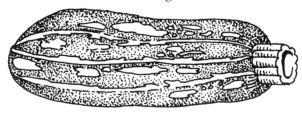

Pizza Tart
Illustrated on page 46

25-cm/10-inch shortcrust pastry case, baked
'blind' (see page 90)
1 egg yolk, lightly beaten

FILLING
6 large ripe tomatoes
olive oil
2 level tablespoons tomato purée
freshly ground black pepper
3 Spanish onions
2 level tablespoons butter
freshly chopped rosemary
2 level tablespoons Parmesan cheese
6-8 thin slices Mozzarella cheese
6-8 thin slices prosciutto
anchovy fillets and stoned black olives

1. Preheat oven to moderate (180°C, 350°F, Gas
Mark 4).

2. To make filling: plunge tomatoes into boiling
water for a minute to loosen skins; peel, seed and
chop them. Heat 4 tablespoons olive oil in a deep
frying pan; add tomatoes, tomato purée, and
freshly ground black pepper, to taste. Simmer over
a low heat until excess moisture is cooked away;
mash occasionally with a wooden spoon to reduce
tomatoes to a purée. Slice onions and simmer them
separately in butter, together with a pinch of
freshly chopped rosemary, until soft and golden,
but do not let them brown.

3. Sprinkle bottom of pastry case with freshly
grated Parmesan cheese. Add onions and cover
with tomato purée. Arrange alternate slices of
Mozzarella cheese and prosciutto around top of
tart. Scatter anchovy fillets and black olives on
cheese and ham. Brush olives and anchovies
lightly with oil.

4. Bake tart for about 20 minutes. Serve hot,
warm or cold as one large tart, cut in wedges, or
in individual tart cases, as a first-rate appetiser or
to hand around with drinks.

53

French Onion Tart

Illustrated on page 46

PÂTE BRISÉE PASTRY
225 g/8 oz plain flour
generous pinch of salt
1 level tablespoon icing sugar
150 g/5 oz butter, softened

ONION FILLING
2 Spanish onions
100 g/4 oz butter
2 level tablespoons flour
3 eggs
150 ml/¼ pint cream
150 ml/¼ pint milk
salt and freshly ground black pepper
freshly grated nutmeg

1. To make pâte brisée: sift flour, salt and sugar into a mixing bowl. Rub in the softened butter with the tips of the fingers until the mixture resembles fine breadcrumbs. Do this very gently and lightly or the mixture will become greasy and heavy. Roll into a ball and chill for 30 minutes or more.

2. To make onion filling: chop onions finely and sauté in butter until transparent. Cool. Add flour, eggs, cream and milk, and mix well. Season to taste with salt, freshly ground black pepper and freshly grated nutmeg.

3. Turn **pâte brisée** on to a floured board and knead or pat pastry lightly into a round. Place in a 25-cm/10-inch pie tin and press out with fingertips to line pie tin (no rolling is necessary). Flute edge of pastry and prick bottom with a fork to avoid air bubbles while cooking. Bake in a hot oven (230°C, 450°F, Gas Mark 8) for 10 minutes. Cool slightly.

4. Pour mixture into pastry case and cook in a moderate oven (160°C, 325°F, Gas Mark 3) for 30 to 40 minutes. Serve very hot.

5. If liked, garnish tart with bacon rolls stuffed with prunes.

Provençal Tomato and Onion Tart

Illustrated on page 47

4 tablespoons olive oil
6 large ripe tomatoes, peeled, seeded and
 chopped
4 level tablespoons tomato purée
1 clove garlic, finely chopped
freshly ground black pepper
3 Spanish onions, sliced
2 level tablespoons butter
freshly chopped rosemary
6-8 level tablespoons Parmesan cheese,
 freshly grated
salt
1 (56-g/2-oz) can anchovy fillets
black olives
olive oil

SAVOURY FINGERTIP PASTRY
225 g/8 oz plain flour
generous pinch of salt
1 level tablespoon icing sugar
150 g/5 oz butter, softened
1 egg yolk
4 tablespoons cold water
lightly beaten egg yolk to glaze

1. To make savoury fingertip pastry: sift flour, salt and sugar into a mixing bowl. Rub in the butter with the tips of the fingers until mixture resembles fine breadcrumbs. Do this very gently and lightly, or mixture will become greasy and heavy. Beat egg yolk and add cold water. Sprinkle over dough and work in lightly with your fingers. Shape moist dough lightly into a flattened round. Wrap in polythene and leave in refrigerator for at least 1 hour to ripen. If chilled dough is too firm for handling, allow to stand at room temperature until it softens slightly. Then turn it on to floured board and roll out as required.

2. Press into pie tin (or individual tins) with your fingers and prick with a fork. Bake 'blind' in a hot oven (230°C, 450°F, Gas Mark 8) for 15 minutes, lower heat to moderate (180°C, 350°F, Gas Mark 4) and bake for 30 minutes. If crust becomes too brown at edges, cover with a little crumpled foil.

3. Line a pie tin with pastry and flute the edge.

Chill. Brush with a little lightly beaten egg yolk and bake in a hot oven (230°C, 450°F, Gas Mark 8) just long enough to set the crust without browning it. Allow to cool.

4. Heat olive oil in a pan; add chopped ripe tomatoes, peeled, seeded and chopped, tomato purée, finely chopped garlic and freshly ground black pepper, to taste. Cook over a low heat until excess moisture is cooked away, mashing occasionally with a wooden spoon to form a purée. Cool.

5. Simmer sliced onions in butter with a little freshly chopped rosemary until soft and golden, but not brown. Cool.

6. Combine tomato purée and onions and add 4–6 level tablespoons freshly grated Parmesan and salt and freshly ground black pepper, to taste.

7. Sprinkle bottom of pastry case with 2 level tablespoons freshly grated Parmesan; cover with tomato and onion mixture. Arrange anchovies in a lattice-work on top and place a black olive in the centre of each square. Brush olives and anchovies lightly with oil and bake in a moderate oven (180°C, 350°F, Gas Mark 4) for about 30 minutes.

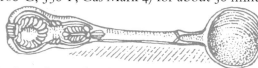

Spinach and Egg Tart
Illustrated on page 46

23- or 25-cm/9- or 10-inch shortcrust pastry case, baked 'blind' (see page 90)
350 g/12 oz frozen spinach, chopped
4 level tablespoons butter
salt and freshly ground black pepper
225 g/8 oz cottage cheese
3 eggs, lightly beaten
25–50 g/1–2 oz Parmesan cheese, freshly grated
8 level tablespoons double cream
freshly grated nutmeg
2 hard-boiled eggs, quartered

1. Sauté chopped spinach in butter for 5 minutes, stirring constantly. Season generously with salt

and freshly ground black pepper, to taste. Drain thoroughly and then add cottage cheese with beaten eggs, freshly grated Parmesan, double cream and grated nutmeg, to taste. Mix well.

2. Spread mixture in pastry case and bake the tart in a moderately hot oven (190°C, 375°F, Gas Mark 5) for 30 minutes or until crust is brown and the cheese custard mixture has set.

3. Garnish with quarters of hard-boiled eggs and serve immediately.

Hot Mushroom Tart
Illustrated on page 46

20-cm/8-inch shortcrust pastry case, baked 'blind' (see page 90)
675 g/1½ lb mushrooms
1 Spanish onion
2 level tablespoons butter
2 tablespoons olive oil
1 level tablespoon flour
300 ml/½ pint single cream
2 eggs, beaten
2 tablespoons dry sherry
salt and freshly ground black pepper

1. Clean and quarter mushrooms; chop onion finely. Sauté mushrooms and onion in butter and olive oil until onion is transparent. Remove a quarter of mushrooms and reserve for garnish. Stir flour into remaining mixture and cook, stirring continuously, for 2 minutes.

2. Combine cream with beaten eggs, sherry and salt and freshly ground black pepper, to taste. Pour over mushroom and onion mixture and stir. Cool.

3. Pour mushroom mixture into prepared pastry case and bake in a moderately hot oven (190°C, 375°F, Gas Mark 5) until brown – about 30 minutes.

4. About 10 minutes before removing tart from oven, scatter reserved mushrooms on top of mushroom mixture. Brush with melted butter and return to oven.

Pasta

56

Spaghetti con Salsa Fredda

450 g/1 lb spaghetti
8 tomatoes, peeled, seeded and diced
2 cloves garlic, finely chopped
16 fresh basil leaves, chopped
4 level tablespoons chopped parsley
4-6 tablespoons warmed olive oil
salt and freshly ground black pepper
freshly grated Parmesan cheese

1. Cook spaghetti in boiling salted water until *al dente* – tender but still firm – about 12 to 15 minutes.

2. Mix together diced tomatoes, chopped garlic, basil and parsley. Moisten with olive oil; season generously with salt and freshly ground black pepper, and serve on drained hot spaghetti with freshly grated Parmesan.

Spaghetti con Pesto

450 g/1 lb spaghetti
salt
butter
freshly grated cheese (Romano or Parmesan)

PESTO SAUCE
2-3 cloves garlic, finely chopped
6-8 level tablespoons finely chopped fresh
   basil
6-8 level tablespoons finely chopped parsley
2-3 level tablespoons pine nuts
6-8 level tablespoons grated cheese
   (Romano or Parmesan)
olive oil
freshly ground black pepper

1. To make Pesto Sauce: pound finely chopped garlic, basil, parsley, pine nuts and grated cheese in a mortar until smooth. Gradually add olive oil and whisk until sauce is smooth and thick. Season to taste with freshly ground black pepper.

2. Cook spaghetti in rapidly boiling salted water until just tender – about 12 to 15 minutes. Drain and place on a hot serving dish. Spoon Pesto Sauce over and serve with a generous knob of butter and grated cheese.

Stuffed Cannelloni

450 g/1 lb flour
1 level teaspoon salt
3 eggs, well-beaten
4-5 tablespoons water
butter
freshly grated Parmesan cheese

FILLING
450 g/1 lb button mushrooms, chopped
225 g/8 oz cooked ham, chopped
1 Spanish onion, chopped
4 level tablespoons butter
2 tablespoons olive oil
4 level tablespoons freshly grated Parmesan
   cheese
4 level tablespoons double cream
salt and freshly ground black pepper
cinnamon

CHEESE SAUCE
2 tablespoons butter
2 tablespoons flour
600 ml/1 pint hot milk
4 tablespoons grated Parmesan cheese
salt and freshly ground black pepper

1. To prepare cannelloni: sift flour and salt into a large mixing bowl. Make a well in the centre and pour in beaten eggs. Add 2 tablespoons water, and mix flour and liquids together with your fingertips until the pasta dough is just soft enough to form into a ball, adding a tablespoon or two of water if the mixture seems too dry. Sprinkle a large pastry board with flour and knead the dough on this board with the flat of your hand until dough is smooth and elastic – about 15 minutes – sifting a little flour on your hand and the board from time to time. Divide dough into 4 equal parts and, using a rolling pin, roll out one piece at a time into paper-thin sheets. To do this, roll out in one direction, stretching the pasta dough as you go, and then roll out in the opposite direction. Sprinkle with flour, fold over and repeat. The dough should be just dry enough not to stick to the rolling pin. Repeat this process of rolling, stretching and folding the dough another 2 or 3 times. Repeat with other pieces of pasta dough. Allow to dry for 1 hour.

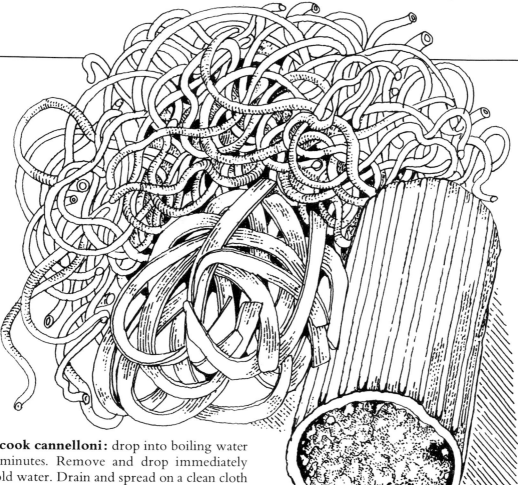

2. To cook cannelloni: drop into boiling water for 5 minutes. Remove and drop immediately into cold water. Drain and spread on a clean cloth to dry.

3. To make filling: sauté chopped mushrooms, ham and onion in butter and olive oil until vegetables are cooked through. Cool. Stir in freshly grated Parmesan, double cream and season to taste with salt, freshly ground black pepper and cinnamon.

4. To make Cheese Sauce: melt butter in the top of a double saucepan. Stir in flour to make a smooth *roux* then add hot milk gradually, stirring continuously. Season to taste with grated Parmesan, salt and freshly ground black pepper. Cook, stirring from time to time, until sauce is smooth and thick.

5. Place 2 tablespoons mushroom filling on each pasta square and roll pasta carefully around filling. Arrange filled cannelloni in a buttered shallow baking dish and cover with Cheese Sauce. Sprinkle generously with grated Parmesan and bake in a moderate oven (180°C, 350°F, Gas Mark 4) for about 30 minutes, or until golden brown.

Green Noodles alla Crema

3.5-4.5 litres/6-8 pints water
450 g/1 lb green noodles
salt
100 g/4 oz butter
100 g/4 oz Parmesan cheese, freshly grated
300 ml/½ pint double cream

1. Bring well-salted water to the boil in a large saucepan. Add green noodles and cook until *al dente* – tender but still firm – about 12 to 15 minutes.

2. While pasta is cooking, melt butter in a saucepan and stir in grated cheese and cream. Cook over a low heat, stirring constantly, until cheese melts and sauce is smooth.

3. Drain noodles and while still very hot, toss with the sauce. Serve noodles with additional grated Parmesan cheese.

58

Lasagne Verdi al Forno

450 g/1 lb green lasagne noodles
salt
butter
225 g/8 oz Mozzarella cheese, diced
50 g/2 oz Parmesan cheese, freshly grated
225 g/8 oz Ricotta cheese, crumbled

MEAT BALLS
450 g/1 lb lean beef, minced
4 eggs
½ loaf stale white bread
1 clove garlic, finely chopped
4 level tablespoons finely chopped parsley
salt and freshly ground black pepper

TOMATO SAUCE
1 Spanish onion, chopped
3 sticks celery, chopped
6 tablespoons olive oil
3 tablespoons tomato purée
1.5 kg/3 lb tomatoes, peeled, seeded and
   chopped
1 teaspoon sugar
2 cloves garlic, chopped
finely chopped parsley
salt and freshly ground black pepper
2 tablespoons butter

1. To make meat balls: combine beef and eggs in a large bowl and mix well. Soak bread in water until soft; squeeze dry and shred. Combine with meat mixture, add garlic and parsley, and season to taste with salt and freshly ground black pepper. Form into marble-sized balls.

2. To make Tomato Sauce: sauté onion and celery in oil in a large frying pan until soft. Transfer to a larger pan and sauté meat balls in remaining fat until golden. Add tomato purée to remaining oil in pan and stir until smooth. Then stir in chopped tomatoes and sugar and cook for 5 minutes, stirring constantly. Press mixture through a fine sieve into a large saucepan. Add chopped garlic and parsley, and simmer mixture for 1 hour. Season with salt and freshly ground black pepper, and add butter. Add meat balls and continue to simmer 30 minutes longer, adding a little water if sauce becomes too thick.

3. Cook the green lasagne, 6 to 8 at a time, in boiling salted water until they are half done; drain carefully. Line a well-buttered baking dish with a layer of lasagne. Remove half the meat balls from the Tomato Sauce with a perforated spoon, and spoon over lasagne. Add a layer of diced Mozzarella cheese, sprinkle generously with grated Parmesan and crumbled Ricotta cheese, and moisten with well-seasoned Tomato Sauce. Repeat, using the same quantities, finishing with Tomato Sauce. Dot with butter and bake in a moderate oven (190°C, 375°F, Gas Mark 5) for about 30 minutes.

Fettuccine alla Capricciosa

100 g/4 oz veal, finely chopped
100 g/4 oz butter
salt and freshly ground black pepper
150 ml/¼ pint red wine
300 ml/½ pint well-flavoured Italian Tomato
   Sauce (see Polenta Pasticciata, page 59)
225 g/8 oz peas
100 g/4 oz fresh or dried mushrooms, sliced
1-2 slices Parma ham, cut in thin strips
450 g/1 lb fettuccine (egg noodles)

1. Sauté finely chopped veal in half the butter until golden. Add salt, freshly ground black pepper and red wine, and simmer gently for 5 to 10 minutes. Add Italian Tomato Sauce and continue cooking over a low heat for 30 minutes.

2. Cook peas in boiling salted water until tender. Drain and sauté with sliced mushrooms and ham in remaining butter until mushrooms are cooked through. Add to sauce.

3. Cook fettuccine in boiling salted water until *al dente* – tender but still firm – about 12 to 15 minutes. Pour sauce over them and serve immediately.

Polenta Pasticciata

450 g/1 lb yellow cornmeal
about 1.25 litres/2–2½ pints salted water
butter
8–10 tablespoons freshly grated Parmesan
    cheese
6–8 level tablespoons breadcrumbs
150 g/5 oz Mozzarella cheese, freshly grated

ITALIAN TOMATO SAUCE
2 Spanish onions, finely chopped
2 cloves garlic, finely chopped
4 tablespoons olive oil
6 level tablespoons Italian tomato purée
1 (793-g/1-lb 12-oz) can Italian peeled
    tomatoes
2 bay leaves
4 level tablespoons finely chopped parsley
¼ level teaspoon oregano
1 small strip lemon peel
6 tablespoons dry white wine
salt and freshly ground black pepper
1–2 tablespoons Worcestershire sauce

1. **To cook polenta:** bring water to the boil.
Pour the cornmeal in slowly, stirring constantly
with a wooden spoon. Continue cooking for 20
to 30 minutes, stirring frequently, until the polenta
is thick and soft and leaves the sides of the pan
easily. Add a little more water if necessary. Stir in
4 tablespoons butter and 6 to 8 tablespoons
freshly grated Parmesan.

2. Butter a shallow baking dish and sprinkle
generously with breadcrumbs and remaining
freshly grated Parmesan. Spread a quarter of the
polenta over it, cover with a quarter of the grated
Mozzarella, and dot with 1 tablespoon butter.
Repeat layers until all the ingredients are used up.

3. Bake in a moderately hot oven (190°C, 375°F,
Gas Mark 5) for 15 to 20 minutes, until well
browned. Serve with well-seasoned Tomato
Sauce.

4. **To make Italian Tomato Sauce:** sauté finely
chopped onions and garlic in olive oil in a large,
thick-bottomed frying pan until transparent and
soft but not coloured. Stir in tomato purée and

continue to cook for a minute or two, stirring
constantly. Pour in peeled tomatoes and add bay
leaves, parsley, oregano and lemon peel. Add dry
white wine, an equal quantity of water, and salt
and freshly ground black pepper, to taste. Simmer
gently, stirring from time to time, for 1 to 2 hours.
Just before serving, stir in Worcestershire sauce,
to taste.

Gnocchi alla Romana
Illustrated on page 68

225 g/8 oz Ricotta or cottage cheese
10–12 tablespoons butter
8 tablespoons freshly grated Parmesan
    cheese
3 egg yolks
4 tablespoons sifted flour
salt and freshly ground black pepper
freshly grated nutmeg

1. Sieve Ricotta or cottage cheese into a mixing
bowl.

2. Beat together 4 tablespoons each melted butter
and grated Parmesan, and 3 egg yolks, and stir
into cheese alternately with flour. Season to taste
with salt, and freshly ground black pepper and
nutmeg.

3. Spoon the mixture into a piping bag fitted with
a large plain nozzle. Hold piping bag over a
large saucepan full of boiling salted water and
force mixture through nozzle, cutting it in 2.5-
cm/1-inch pieces (gnocchi) with scissors. Cook
gnocchi for 6 or 7 minutes. Remove with a
perforated spoon and drain on a clean cloth.

4. When ready to serve, arrange gnocchi in over-
lapping rows in a well-buttered shallow casserole
or *gratin* dish. Pour 6 to 8 tablespoons melted
butter over them and sprinkle with remaining
Parmesan cheese. Bake in a moderate oven
(180°C, 350°F, Gas Mark 4) for 10 minutes, and
then brown under grill until golden.

Rice

Basic Italian Risotto *Serves 4 to 6*
Risotto con Funghi *Serves 4 to 6*
Saffron Rice with Avocado *Serves 4 to 6*

60

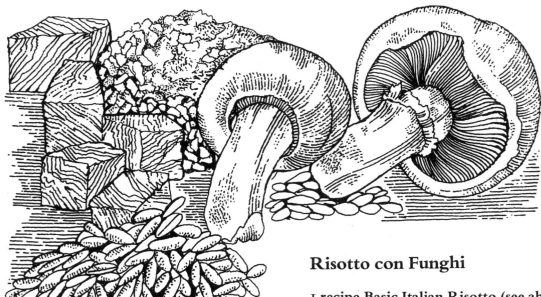

Basic Italian Risotto

½ **Spanish onion, finely chopped**
4 tablespoons butter
350 g/12 oz rice
1–1.5 litres/1½–2 pints hot beef stock
½ **level teaspoon powdered saffron**
salt and freshly ground black pepper
freshly grated Parmesan cheese

1. Place chopped onion in a deep saucepan with butter. Cook slowly for 2 to 4 minutes, taking care that the onion does not become brown.

2. Add rice and cook over medium heat, stirring constantly with a wooden spoon. After a minute or so, stir in a cup of hot beef stock in which you have dissolved the powdered saffron.

3. Continue cooking, adding stock as needed and stirring from time to time, until rice is cooked – 15 to 18 minutes. Correct seasoning. By this time all the stock in the pan should have been absorbed by the rice, leaving rice tender but still moist. Serve immediately with extra butter and freshly grated Parmesan.

Risotto con Funghi

1 recipe Basic Italian Risotto (see above)
6–8 dried mushrooms
225 g/8 oz cooked ham, diced
6–8 level tablespoons freshly grated
   Parmesan cheese
butter

1. Soak dried mushrooms for several hours in hot water. Drain, cut into small pieces and combine with diced cooked ham.

2. Fold ham and mushroom mixture carefully into *risotto* cooked as in Basic Italian Risotto. Then stir in freshly grated Parmesan cheese.

3. Place rice in a well-buttered casserole. Cover and cook in a moderate oven (180°C, 350°F, Gas Mark 4) for about 20 minutes. Serve immediately.

Saffron Rice with Avocado

½ **teaspoon powdered saffron**
6 tablespoons dry white wine
900 ml/1½ pints hot chicken stock
350 g/12 oz rice
salt and freshly ground black pepper
1 ripe avocado pear
juice of 1 lemon

1. Dissolve saffron in white wine. Add it to hot chicken stock and combine in a large saucepan with rice, salt and freshly ground black pepper, to taste.

2. Cover pan and simmer until all the liquid is absorbed and the rice is tender.

3. Cut avocado pear in half, lengthwise. Remove stone. Brush cut sides with lemon juice. Peel avocado with a sharp knife. Brush again with lemon juice to preserve colour. Dice avocado into a small bowl. Sprinkle with remaining lemon juice. Add salt and freshly ground black pepper, to taste. Toss well.

4. Transfer saffron rice to a heated bowl; garnish with diced avocado and serve immediately.

Chicken Liver Pilaff

butter
2 level tablespoons finely chopped onion
175 g/6 oz rice
600 ml/1 pint chicken stock
pinch of saffron
4 level tablespoons sultanas
salt and freshly ground black pepper
225 g/8 oz chicken livers
1 level tablespoon flour
300 ml/½ pint well-flavoured Brown Sauce
   (see page 83)
4 tablespoons Madeira wine

1. To prepare pilaff: melt 1 tablespoon butter in a thick-bottomed saucepan and simmer finely chopped onion for a minute or two. Add the rice and stir until rice is well coated with butter. Do not let it colour. Add the stock, saffron and sultanas, and season to taste with salt and freshly ground black pepper. Cover saucepan and simmer rice gently for 15 minutes, or until tender. Correct seasoning. Lightly stir in 1 tablespoon butter and press into well-buttered ring mould. Bake in a moderate oven (180°C, 350°F, Gas Mark 4) for 5 minutes.

2. To prepare chicken livers: cut green parts from livers. Wash livers carefully and pat dry in a clean cloth. Dice livers and toss them lightly in seasoned flour. Sauté in 2 tablespoons butter until

lightly browned. Pour in Brown Sauce and wine; season with salt and freshly ground black pepper. Simmer for a few more minutes, or until tender.

3. Turn rice ring out on a hot serving platter and fill with chicken livers.

Arancini
Illustrated on page 68

100 g/4 oz chicken livers, chopped
1 Spanish onion, finely chopped
1 clove garlic, finely chopped
4 tablespoons olive oil
salt and freshly ground black pepper
4–6 level tablespoons tomato purée
150 ml/¼ pint dry white wine
350 g/8 oz rice
butter
6–8 level tablespoons freshly grated
   Parmesan cheese
2 egg yolks, well beaten
2 eggs, well beaten
dried breadcrumbs
fat for deep-frying

1. Sauté chopped chicken livers, onion and garlic in olive oil until vegetables are transparent. Season to taste with salt and freshly ground black pepper. Add tomato purée diluted with dry white wine. Add enough water to make a creamy sauce, cover saucepan and simmer gently for 30 minutes.

2. Boil or steam rice in usual way until tender but not mushy. Drain well, butter lightly and season to taste with freshly grated Parmesan. Add well-beaten egg yolks and mix well.

3. Strain sauce from chicken livers into rice and mix well.

4. Form small balls the size of golf balls with seasoned rice mixture; then with your forefinger, dig a hole in the centre of each ball and put 1 teaspoon of liver mixture into each. Pinch shut and re-roll ball. Chill.

5. When ready to fry: dip *arancini* in beaten eggs and then in breadcrumbs, and fry until golden.

61

Terrines and Pâtés

62

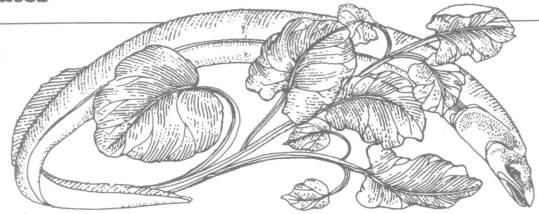

Terrine d'Anguilles
Illustrated on page 65

1 kg/2 lb fresh eel, skinned, boned and
   filleted
675 g/1½ lb whiting, skinned and filleted
450 g/1 lb sole, skinned and filleted
150 ml/¼ pint milk
salt and freshly ground black pepper
3 slices white bread
2 egg whites
750 ml/1¼ pints double cream
1 bunch watercress
parsley
dry white wine
butter

EEL JELLY
reserved eel bones
reserved eel stock
1 leaf gelatine
1 egg white
watercress or parsley stems

TO DECORATE
2 canned red pimientos
12 watercress leaves

CRÈME AU CRESSON
2 bunches watercress, with stems removed
salt
150 ml/¼ pint double cream
juice of 1 lemon or lime
freshly ground black pepper

1. Ask your fishmonger to kill and skin eel and
cut it into fillets. Ask him for the bones. (You'll
have to order your eel several days in advance.)

2. Cut eel fillets into even-sized pieces just long
enough to fit into a large oval deep pie dish.
Combine whiting, sole and the eel trimmings and
put through finest blade of your mincer twice.
Put mixture in a bowl and refrigerate for 1½ hours.

3. **To make panade:** bring milk to the boil in a
small saucepan. Season generously with salt and
freshly ground black pepper and remove from
heat. Trim crusts from three slices white bread
and shred into hot milk. Return pan to the heat
and bring to the boil again. Cool panade mixture.

4. **To make mousseline:** squeeze excess liquid
from panade mixture and beat into fish mousse.
Then beat in egg whites, one by one. When
mixture is smooth and thoroughly blended, place
bowl in a larger bowl containing ice, and gradually beat in double cream. Season to taste with
salt and freshly ground black pepper and refrigerate mousseline for 1½ hours to 'ripen' flavours.

5. **To test for flavour:** roll 2 tablespoons of the
mousseline mixture into a ball and place gently in
a saucepan with enough simmering water to just
cover it. Simmer it for a few minutes as you would
a *quenelle* until it is puffed and floats to the surface.
Cool and taste to see if you need to add a little
more seasoning.

6. **To prepare eel fillets:** remove stems from
bunch of watercress and the same amount of
parsley. Place stems and eel fillets in a flameproof
porcelainised shallow casserole or frying pan. Add
enough dry white wine to cover and bring gently
to the boil. Allow to gently bubble in the wine
for 2 minutes only. Remove pan from heat and
cool eel fillets in the stock.

7. To assemble terrine: generously butter a large deep oval pie dish or *terrine* (to hold 1 kg/ 2 lb *pâté*). Place a third of mousseline mixture in the bottom of the pie dish or *terrine*, gently spreading about 5 mm/¼ inch of the mixture around the sides of the dish. Chop parsley and watercress leaves and spread them on a large plate. Remove eel fillets from stock (reserving stock for later use) and roll fillets in the chopped herbs. Arrange half of the herbed eel fillets on the bed of mousseline mixture in the dish. Sprinkle with half of remaining chopped herbs, top with a third of the mousseline mixture and arrange remaining eel fillets on this bed. Sprinkle with remaining chopped herbs as above, and cover with remaining mousseline mixture.

8. Cover pie dish or *terrine* lightly with a double thickness of aluminium foil, then cover with a plate (or a folded wet tea towel). Place covered *terrine* in a roasting tin half filled with boiling water and cook for 1¾ hours in a cool oven (150°C, 300°F, Gas Mark 2).

9. Remove *terrine* from oven. Allow to cool and then place in the refrigerator for 24 hours.

10. To make eel jelly: place reserved eel bones in the stock and allow to bubble gently for 10 minutes only. Cool stock to lukewarm and add leaf gelatine to 'strengthen' jelly. Clarify the stock by boiling it for 3 minutes with the egg white and 4 to 6 stems of watercress or parsley. Strain through a fine muslin into a bowl and reserve for use.

11. To decorate terrine: cut 12 little diamonds from canned red pimiento. Blanch watercress leaves by placing them in cold water to cover and bring them to the boil. Drain. Remove *terrine* from the refrigerator. Spoon over enough clarified jelly (melt jelly by placing bowl in a pan of hot water) to just cover top of mousseline lightly. Allow to set, then decorate *terrine* with a ring of alternating pimiento 'diamonds' and watercress leaves. Gently spoon over enough of the jelly to keep leaves in place. **Note:** If any are displaced during this operation re-form pattern and allow to set, before brushing a final time with jelly. Return to refrigerator to set.

12. To make Crème au Cresson: place watercress leaves in blender with a generous pinch of salt. Blend at high speed for 1 second. Add double cream and blend for 1 second more. Then add lemon or lime juice, and salt and freshly ground black pepper, to taste. Blend for 1 second more. Serve in a sauceboat.

13. To serve terrine: cut in thin slices and serve cold with *Crème au Cresson*.

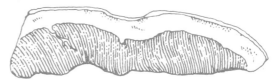

Terrine aux Foies de Volaille

225 g/8 oz lean pork
225 g/8 oz fat bacon
175 g/6 oz poultry livers
2 cloves garlic
4 small shallots
4 eggs, beaten
2 level tablespoons cornflour
3 tablespoons dry white wine
4 tablespoons Cointreau
salt and freshly ground black pepper
freshly grated nutmeg
1 sprig thyme
1 bay leaf
**Madeira Aspic (see Basic Meat Aspic,
   page 84)**

1. Put lean pork, fat bacon, poultry livers (chicken or duck, or a combination of the two) through the finest blade of your mincer, together with garlic and shallots. Combine mixture in a large bowl with beaten eggs, cornflour, dry white wine, Cointreau, and salt, freshly ground black pepper and grated nutmeg, to taste. Mix well.

2. Place a sprig of thyme, a bay leaf and the *pâté* mixture in an earthenware *terrine*. Cover the *terrine*, place in a pan of water and cook in a moderate oven (160°C to 180°C, 325°F to 350°F, Gas Mark 3 to 4) for about 1½ hours. At the end of the cooking, add Madeira Aspic.

The addition of Cointreau in this recipe removes any bitterness from the poultry livers.

Terrine of Pheasant

1 medium-sized pheasant
1 small onion, sliced
2 small carrots, sliced
2 sprigs parsley
1 bay leaf
salt
pinch of thyme
75 ml/3 fl oz Madeira
75 ml/3 fl oz cognac
225 g/8 oz fresh lean pork
450 g/1 lb fresh fat pork
1 egg, beaten
½ clove garlic, crushed
freshly ground black pepper
Madeira Aspic (see Basic Meat Aspic,
    page 84)

1. Split pheasant down the back. Open it out flat and cut the meat from each breast into strips. Place strips in a bowl with sliced onion, carrots, parsley, bay leaf, ½ teaspoon salt, a pinch of thyme, Madeira and cognac. Let meat marinate in this mixture for 2 hours, then drain. Strain marinade, reserving juices.

2. Cut remaining meat from the pheasant, and combine with lean pork and half the fat pork. Chop finely; add beaten egg, crushed garlic, ½ teaspoon salt, freshly ground black pepper, to taste, and the reserved marinade. Blend until very smooth.

3. Line a *terrine* or earthenware casserole with thin strips of remaining fat pork, thinly sliced. Spread a third of the meat mixture over the bottom, and arrange marinated strips on it. Add alternate layers of meat mixture and marinated strips. Then add alternate layers of meat mixture and breast mixture, finishing with the meat mixture.

4. Cover casserole. Place it in a pan of hot water and bake in a moderately hot oven (200°C, 400°F, Gas Mark 6) for about 1½ hours. Remove cover and place a weighted plate on the *terrine* to compress it gently as it cools.

5. When cold, unmould *terrine* and turn out on a board. Scrape fat from surface. Wash and dry casserole, then return *terrine* to it, bottom side up. Pour Madeira Aspic around it, cooled but still liquid, and chill until set.

Pâté of Duck

1 tender duckling
450 g/1 lb veal
225 g/8 oz bacon, diced
4 level tablespoons savoury biscuit or
    cracker crumbs
salt and freshly ground black pepper
freshly grated nutmeg
1 egg, well beaten
1 glass dry sherry
100 g/4 oz thinly sliced bacon
1 onion, thinly sliced
1 lemon, thinly sliced
1 bay leaf
flour and water paste

1. Bone a tender duckling and cut the flesh into small pieces. Dice veal roughly, removing skin. Put veal, diced bacon and duck trimmings through the finest blade of your mincer twice to make a fine *farce*.

2. Add biscuit or cracker crumbs. Season to taste with salt, freshly ground black pepper and a little nutmeg, and moisten with well-beaten egg and sherry. Mix thoroughly.

3. Line a *terrine* with sliced bacon. Put in a layer of the *farce*, then some pieces of duck, more *farce*, and so on, until the dish is full. Cover with sliced bacon, and top with thin slices of onion and lemon, and a bay leaf. Put on the lid and seal the join with a paste made of flour and water. Bake in a moderate oven (180°C, 350°F, Gas Mark 4) for 1½ to 2 hours, until the pieces of duck feel quite tender when they are pierced with a skewer. (Remove pastry seal after 1½ hours to check on this.) Remove lid of *terrine* and place a weighted plate on the *pâté* to compress it gently as it cools. Chill in refrigerator for 2 to 3 days before serving.

Terrine d'Anguilles (see page 62)
Pâté aux Herbes (see page 71)

Fondant de Volaille 'Auberge du Père Bise'
(see page 69)

Arancini (see page 61)

Gnocchi alla Romana (see page 59)

Fondant de Volaille 'Auberge du Père Bise'

Illustrated on page 67

1 large capon (about 1.5 kg/3½ lb)
300 ml/½ pint dry sherry
2 tablespoons cognac
6-8 tablespoons Noilly
4 sprigs of thyme
1 bay leaf
4 sprigs of parsley
2 tablespoons port
4 shallots
2 carrots
½ Spanish onion
2 cloves garlic
6-8 peppercorns
225 g/8 oz pork fat
450 g/1 lb lean pork
2 level tablespoons coarse salt
freshly ground black pepper
225 g/8 oz foie gras
25 g/1 oz pistachio nuts
thin strips pork fat (about 450 g/1 lb)
diced foie gras (optional)
salted flour and water paste

1. Skin chicken and remove meat from bones, leaving breasts whole.

2. In a large porcelain bowl, combine sherry, cognac and Noilly with herbs, port, shallots, carrots and onions, all finely chopped, and garlic and peppercorns. Add chicken pieces and marinate in this mixture for at least 12 hours.

3. Dice pork fat and half the lean pork, and combine with coarse salt, and freshly ground black pepper, to taste. Refrigerate for 6 hours to prevent meat changing colour during cooking. Pass through the finest blade of your mincer.

4. Place chicken pieces in a roasting tin with remaining pork, diced, and roast in a hot oven (230°C, 450°F, Gas Mark 8) for 5 minutes, or until meat has coloured slightly. Strain marinade juices over meat and cook for 5 minutes more.

5. Remove chicken breasts and pass the remaining chicken pieces and pork juices through the finest

blade of your mincer, blending in *foie gras* at the same time. Combine minced pork and pork fat with chicken mixture. Stir in pistachio nuts and remaining marinade juices, and place *pâté* mixture in refrigerator to 'relax' for 2 to 3 hours.

6. When ready to cook: line a large *terrine* or *pâté* mould with paper-thin strips of pork fat; fill a quarter full with *pâté* mixture; scatter diced *foie gras* over this for a really luxurious *terrine*, as served at Père Bise; cover with a layer of *pâté* mixture and place marinated chicken breasts on this. Repeat alternate layers of *pâté* mixture and diced *foie gras*, ending with *pâté* mixture. Top with thin strips of pork fat. Cover *terrine* and seal edges with a dough made of flour, water and salt, so that no moisture escapes. Place *terrine* in a pan of boiling water and bake in a moderate oven (160°C, 325°F, Gas Mark 3) for 1 hour. Keep *pâté* in refrigerator for 2 to 3 days before serving.

Home-made Pâté

225 g/8 oz cooked beef, lamb or veal
175 g/6 oz sausagemeat
2 slices white bread, trimmed
little milk
2 shallots, finely chopped
1 small onion, finely chopped
4 level tablespoons finely chopped parsley
2 egg yolks
salt and freshly ground black pepper
butter
gherkins or well-flavoured French Tomato
    Sauce (see page 83)

1. Put cooked beef, lamb or veal through a mincer with sausagemeat.

2. Soak bread in a little milk and squeeze almost dry. Add soaked bread to meat with finely chopped shallots, onion and parsley. Add egg yolks, and salt and freshly ground black pepper, to taste, and spoon mixture into a well-buttered *pâté* mould. Cook in a moderate oven (180°C, 350°F, Gas Mark 4) for 1 hour.

3. Serve cold with gherkins, or hot with well-flavoured French Tomato Sauce.

70

Terrine of Hare

675 g/1½ lb hare meat
butter
salt and freshly ground black pepper
pinch of nutmeg
2 level teaspoons finely chopped fresh thyme
   or 1 level teaspoon dried thyme
2 level tablespoons finely chopped parsley
150 ml/¼ pint dry white wine
2 tablespoons brandy
450 g/1 lb smoothly ground sausagemeat
slices of fat bacon
flour and water paste

1. Any remains of uncooked hare may be used to make a *terrine*. Remove all bones, trim the flesh and cut it in small pieces, and then weigh it.

2. Melt butter in a saucepan and sauté hare for a minute or two to stiffen outside; do not brown.

3. Place meat in a shallow bowl with salt, freshly ground black pepper and nutmeg, to taste, finely chopped thyme and parsley, and dry white wine and brandy. Marinate hare in this mixture for at least 2 hours.

4. The sausagemeat used should be very fine and smooth. If not sufficiently smooth when bought, put it through the mincer; pound it well and then sieve it.

5. Combine sausagemeat with the marinade liquids and the blood from the hare, if there is any, or the liver, pounded and sieved, to give the forcemeat the taste and darkish colour of the game. Mix well. Add marinated hare and mix again.

6. Line the bottom and sides of a *terrine* with thin slices of fat bacon, then put in the mixture, which should fill it, forming a mound on the top. Cover the top with more fat bacon and put on the lid. Seal round the join of lid and pot with a thick paste made of flour and water to keep in all the flavour of the meat while it is cooking. Make sure, however, that the little hole in the top of the lid is left open, or the *terrine* will burst in the cooking. If there is no hole in the lid, leave a small piece of the join unsealed.

7. To cook terrine: place it in a deepish pan with a little cold water round it and bring this to the boil over the heat. Then place it in the oven and cook until the meat is ready – 2 to 2½ hours. The water round the *terrine* should be kept boiling all the time; if it boils away, add more boiling water. Test the meat by running a needle in through the hole in the top, or if, on removing the cover, the fat on top looks quite clear and the meat moves about easily without adhering to the bottom and sides, it is sufficiently cooked. Remove cover and place a weighted plate on the *terrine* to compress it gently as it cools. Chill in the refrigerator for at least 3 days before serving to allow flavours to ripen.

To keep terrine: a *terrine* like this will keep for 2 to 3 months in the refrigerator if sealed with a layer of melted lard. Other kinds of game may be used instead of hare.

Chicken Liver Terrine

575 g/1¼ lb fresh chicken livers
6 tablespoons port
generous pinch of thyme
4 bay leaves
4 slices ham
350 g/12 oz sausagemeat
3 slices bread
little milk
150 ml/¼ pint dry white wine
½ clove garlic, finely chopped
freshly ground black pepper
thin rashers streaky bacon, or bacon and
   pork fat
melted lard

1. Place fresh chicken livers in a bowl, add port, a generous pinch of thyme, and 2 bay leaves, crumbled. Allow the livers to marinate in this mixture for at least 2 hours.

2. Put three-quarters of the chicken livers through a mincer with ham, sausagemeat, and bread which you have soaked in a little milk. Stir in dry white wine to make a rather wet mixture. Then add finely chopped garlic and freshly ground black pepper, to taste. Mix well.

3. Line a *pâté* mould with thin rashers of streaky bacon. For a more subtle flavour, ask your butcher to give you paper-thin strips of larding pork fat. Place the strips between 2 sheets of waxed paper, and pound them as thinly as possible. Then use thin strips of pork fat alternately with strips of streaky bacon to line your *pâté* mould.

4. Spread half of the liver and sausage mixture in the bottom of the mould. Add whole chicken livers, and cover with remaining liver and sausage mixture.

5. Top with thin strips of bacon and 2 bay leaves. Cover mould, place in a pan of boiling water and cook in a moderately hot oven (190°C, 375°F, Gas Mark 5) for $1\frac{1}{4}$ to $1\frac{1}{2}$ hours. Place a weight on *pâté* – all excess juices will pour over edges of mould – and allow to cool. When cold, coat with a little melted lard. Chill in refrigerator for 2 to 3 days before serving.

Pâté aux Herbes
Illustrated on page 65

450 g/1 lb pork
450 g/1 lb fresh or 100 g/4 oz frozen leaf
  spinach
salt
100 g/4 oz cooked ham
100 g/4 oz green bacon
100 g/4 oz cooked ox tongue
1 Spanish onion, finely chopped
2 cloves garlic, finely chopped
4 level tablespoons finely chopped basil
4 level tablespoons finely chopped parsley
4 level tablespoons finely chopped chervil
4 leaves rosemary, finely chopped
4 eggs, beaten
freshly ground black pepper
cayenne
freshly grated nutmeg
100 g/4 oz chicken livers
2 level tablespoons butter
150 ml/$\frac{1}{4}$ pint double cream
2 level tablespoons powdered gelatine
strips of pork fat
gherkins

1. Put pork through finest blade of mincer.

2. Cook spinach in boiling salted water for 5 minutes. Drain and press dry with hands to remove all water. Chop coarsely and put through mincer with pork again.

3. Dice ham, green bacon and ox tongue and combine with finely chopped onion, garlic and fresh herbs. (If you use dried herbs, use only half the quantity.) Stir in beaten eggs and add salt, freshly ground black pepper, cayenne and nutmeg to taste.

4. Chop chicken livers and sauté in 2 tablespoons butter until golden. Stir in cream and powdered gelatine which you have dissolved in a little water and mix well. Add to *pâté* mixture and mix well.

5. Line the bottom and sides of an ovenproof *terrine* with thin strips of pork fat. Press *pâté* mixture into *terrine*, cover with thin strips of pork fat and cook in a moderate oven (160°C, 325°F, Gas Mark 3) for 30 minutes. Lower heat to 150°C, 300°F, Gas Mark 2 and cook for another 30 to 40 minutes.

6. Remove from oven and cool. Serve cold, cut into slices, with gherkins.

Soups

72

Fresh Lettuce Soup I

2 lettuces
225 g/8 oz spinach leaves
6 spring onions
4 level tablespoons butter
1.15 litres/2 pints well-flavoured chicken
   stock
salt and freshly ground black pepper
1 egg yolk
4-6 level tablespoons double cream
fried croûtons of bread

1. Remove hard stalks and discoloured leaves from lettuce and spinach. Wash the leaves well and drain. Trim roots and most of the green from onions. Slice vegetables thinly.

2. Melt butter in a saucepan and simmer sliced vegetables gently for 15 minutes, stirring from time to time. Add stock and bring to the boil. Reduce heat, cover and simmer gently for 35 minutes. Correct seasoning.

3. Whisk egg yolk and cream in a soup tureen. Add hot soup, stirring all the time. Serve with *croûtons*.

Fresh Lettuce Soup II

2 lettuces
225 g/8 oz spinach leaves
3-4 spring onions
4 level tablespoons butter
600 ml/1 pint well-flavoured chicken stock
salt and freshly ground black pepper
300 ml/½ pint Béchamel Sauce (see page 84)
150 ml/¼ pint cream
4 level tablespoons finely chopped chervil
   or parsley
fried croûtons of bread

1. Remove hard stalks and discoloured leaves from lettuce and spinach. Wash the leaves well and drain. Trim roots and most of the green from onions. Slice vegetables thinly.

2. Melt butter in a saucepan and simmer sliced vegetables gently for 15 minutes, stirring from time to time. Add stock and bring to the boil. Reduce heat, cover and simmer gently for 35 minutes. Correct seasoning.

3. Add Béchamel Sauce and simmer for 10 minutes. Press through a fine sieve or blend in an electric blender. Return purée to a clean saucepan. Stir over a high heat until boiling. Add cream and chervil or parsley, and serve with *croûtons*.

Chicken Soup with Matzoh Balls *Serves 4 to 6*
Chilled Spanish Soup *Serves 6 to 8*
Potage à la Bonne Femme *Serves 4 to 6*

Chicken Soup with Matzoh Balls

1.4 litres/2½ pints well-seasoned chicken
  stock

MATZOH BALLS
2 egg yolks
½ teaspoon salt
2 tablespoons melted chicken fat
4 level tablespoons finely chopped parsley
4 level tablespoons matzoh meal
2 egg whites, stiffly beaten

1. **To make matzoh balls:** beat egg yolks until
light. Add salt and melted chicken fat, and beat
again. Add finely chopped parsley and matzoh
meal, and mix well. Then fold in beaten egg
whites thoroughly. Chill dough for 15 minutes
and form into very small balls.

2. Drop balls into boiling stock, cover and simmer
for 20 minutes, or until tender.

Chilled Spanish Soup

Illustrated on page 85

2 slices white bread
8 large ripe tomatoes
1 cucumber
900 ml/1½ pints chicken broth, chilled
1 level teaspoon salt
freshly ground black pepper
2 tablespoons olive oil
2 tablespoons lemon juice
1-2 cloves garlic, finely chopped
4-6 level tablespoons finely chopped parsley
garlic croûtons
1 green pepper, seeded and chopped
4-6 spring onions, finely chopped
2 hard-boiled eggs, finely chopped

1. Trim crusts from bread and soak in cold water.

2. Peel, seed and chop tomatoes. Peel, seed and
dice cucumber.

3. Combine chopped vegetables (saving half the
tomatoes and a little cucumber for garnish) with
soaked bread and well-flavoured chilled chicken

broth. Season to taste with salt, freshly ground
black pepper, olive oil, lemon juice and finely
chopped garlic and parsley. Purée in an electric
blender or pass through a fine sieve. Chill.

4. Serve with small accompanying bowls of
garlic *croûtons*, finely chopped green pepper,
spring onions, tomatoes, cucumber and hard-
boiled eggs.

Potage à la Bonne Femme

4 level tablespoons butter
4-5 spring onions, thinly sliced
1 lettuce, shredded
½ cucumber, peeled, seeded and sliced into
  matchsticks
1 (227-g/8-oz) packet frozen peas
4-5 sprigs tarragon, chervil or sorrel, finely
  chopped
1.15 litres/2 pints chicken stock
2 egg yolks
150 ml/¼ pint cream
salt and freshly ground black pepper
fried bread croûtons

1. Melt butter in a saucepan. Add vegetables and
herbs and simmer gently for about 5 minutes.

2. Bring chicken stock to the boil. Pour it over the
vegetables and allow the soup to simmer gently
for about 30 minutes, or until vegetables are
quite tender.

3. Beat egg yolks and cream with a fork until well
blended. Remove pan from the heat and strain
egg and cream mixture into the soup, stirring
constantly.

4. Return pan to heat and simmer, stirring constantly, until the yolks thicken, but do not let it
come to the boil or your soup will curdle. Season
to taste with salt and freshly ground black pepper.
Serve with *croûtons*.

73

74

Hollandaise Soup

1 small turnip, diced
2 carrots, diced
½ cucumber, peeled, seeded and diced
1 (227-g/8-oz) packet frozen peas
2 level tablespoons butter
2 level tablespoons flour
1.15 litres/2 pints well-flavoured chicken
   stock
2 egg yolks
150 ml/¼ pint single cream
1 level tablespoon finely chopped parsley
   or tarragon
pinch of sugar
salt and freshly ground black pepper

1. Cook vegetables in separate saucepans of boiling salted water until just tender. Drain.

2. Melt the butter in a saucepan. Add the flour and cook, stirring with a wooden spoon, until smooth. Pour in the stock and simmer, stirring constantly, until soup is slightly thickened. Skim if necessary.

3. Remove saucepan from heat. Mix egg yolks and cream together and strain into soup, stirring constantly. Simmer gently over a low heat until the yolks thicken, but do not allow the soup to boil again or it will curdle.

4. Just before serving: add the chopped parsley or tarragon and a pinch of sugar, and season to taste with salt and freshly ground black pepper. Put the prepared vegetables into a hot soup tureen, pour the soup over them and serve immediately.

Crème Germiny

4 leaves sorrel
2 level tablespoons butter
600 ml/1 pint well-flavoured chicken
   consommé
8 egg yolks
4 level tablespoons double cream
salt and freshly ground black pepper

1. Wash and drain sorrel; shred finely. Simmer gently in butter until soft. Add chicken consommé and bring to the boil.

2. Combine egg yolks, double cream, and salt and freshly ground black pepper, to taste, in a large mixing bowl, and whisk with an egg beater until smooth. Pour hot consommé on to the egg mixture and mix well.

3. Pour mixture into a clean saucepan and simmer gently over a very low heat, stirring constantly, until smooth and thick. Do not let soup come to the boil or it will curdle.

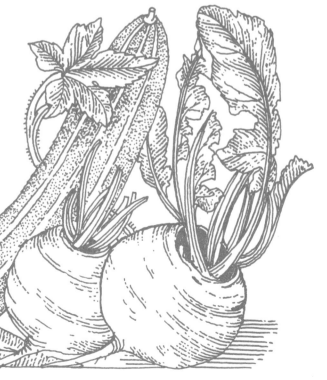

Fresh Mushroom Soup

4 level tablespoons butter
3 level tablespoons flour
600 ml/1 pint chicken stock
300 ml/½ pint milk
225 g/8 oz mushrooms, washed and sieved
4 level tablespoons chopped parsley
juice of 1 lemon
150 ml/¼ pint double cream
salt and freshly ground black pepper

1. Melt butter in a saucepan. Add flour and cook gently for 3 to 4 minutes.

2. Add chicken stock; blend well and bring to the boil, stirring all the time. Add milk, sieved mushrooms, parsley and lemon juice, and cook for 5 minutes.

3. Stir in cream and season to taste with salt and freshly ground black pepper. Serve hot or cold.

Chilled Asparagus Soup

Illustrated on page 86

1 bunch fresh asparagus
¼ Spanish onion, finely chopped
4 tablespoons plus 450 ml/¾ pint chicken stock
4 level tablespoons butter
2 level tablespoons flour
salt and freshly ground black pepper
300 ml/½ pint double cream
2 level tablespoons finely chopped parsley
grated rind of ½ lemon

1. Cut the tips off asparagus and reserve for garnish. Break off tough white ends. Wash stalks and slice into 2.5-cm/1-inch segments.

2. Combine segments in a saucepan with finely chopped onion, 4 tablespoons chicken stock and butter, and simmer, covered, until tender.

3. Remove cooked asparagus segments. Stir in flour until well blended, add remaining chicken stock and cook, stirring continuously, until soup reaches boiling point. Season to taste with salt and freshly ground black pepper.

4. Return asparagus segments to thickened soup and purée in an electric blender or press through a fine sieve. Allow to cool, then chill.

5. Just before serving: add double cream and garnish with asparagus tips which you have cooked until tender and then chilled. Sprinkle with finely chopped parsley and grated lemon rind.

75

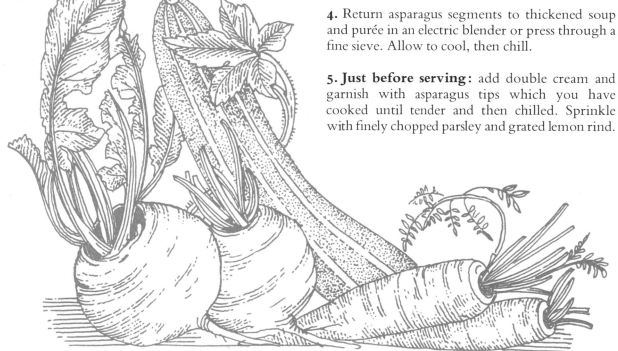

Provençal Fish Salad

300 ml/½ pint well-flavoured mayonnaise
   (see page 89)
1 clove garlic, finely chopped
1-2 anchovy fillets, finely chopped
2 level tablespoons finely chopped basil or
   tarragon
2 level tablespoons finely chopped parsley
1-2 level tablespoons finely chopped capers
lemon juice, to taste
675 g/1½ lb cold poached fish, diced
lettuce leaves
finely chopped parsley
black olives

1. Combine first 7 ingredients; toss diced cold poached fish lightly in sauce until well coated.

2. Arrange lettuce leaves around edges of a large shallow salad bowl; pile fish mixture into centre of bowl and garnish with finely chopped parsley and black olives.

Brandade de Morue (Cream of Salt Cod)

Illustrated on page 88

450 g/1 lb salt cod fillets (smoked haddock
   fillets make a delicious alternative)
1-2 cloves garlic, crushed
150 ml/¼ pint double cream
150 ml/¼ pint olive oil
1-2 boiled potatoes (optional)
juice and finely grated rind of ½ lemon
freshly ground black pepper
bread triangles fried in butter

1. Soak cod fillets overnight in a bowl under gently running water. Drain, put salt cod in a saucepan, cover with cold water and bring to the boil. Drain and return to pan. Cover with cold water and bring to the boil again. Turn off heat and allow to steep in hot water for 10 minutes. Strain cod, remove skin and bones, and flake fish with a fork.

2. Place cod fillets in electric blender with crushed garlic, 2 tablespoons cream and 4 tablespoons olive oil, and blend (or work mixture to a smooth paste with a mortar and pestle), from time to time adding remainder of cream and olive oil alternately until they are completely absorbed and the *brandade* has the consistency of puréed potatoes. If mixture is too salty, add more potatoes, to taste.

3. Simmer mixture in a double saucepan or over water until heated through. Stir in lemon juice and grated peel, and season to taste with freshly ground black pepper.

Note: *Brandade de morue* may be served hot or cold. If hot, place in a mound on a warm serving dish and surround with bread triangles fried in butter.

Brandade de Saumon

675 g/1 lb fresh salmon
100 g/4 oz smoked salmon, chopped
1 clove garlic, crushed
150 ml/¼ pint double cream
150 ml/¼ pint olive oil
lemon juice
Tabasco sauce
salt and freshly ground black pepper
bread triangles fried in olive oil or butter

1. Poach salmon until tender. Remove from water, drain and flake, removing bones and skin.

2. Place salmon flakes and chopped smoked salmon in electric blender with crushed garlic, 2 tablespoons cream and 4 tablespoons olive oil, and blend, adding remainder of cream and olive oil alternately from time to time, until the oil and cream are completely absorbed and the *brandade* is creamy smooth.

3. When ready to serve: simmer mixture in top of a double saucepan. Stir in lemon juice and Tabasco, to taste, and season generously with salt and freshly ground black pepper.

Note: *Brandade de saumon* may be served hot or cold. If hot, place in a mound on a warm serving dish and surround with bread triangles fried in olive oil or butter.

Maquereaux en Court-Bouillon

Illustrated on page 87

6 small mackerel
½ lemon, thinly sliced
4 carrots, scraped and diced
1 Spanish onion, diced
1 green pepper, seeded and diced
2 sprigs thyme
2 bay leaves
8 black peppercorns
4 cloves
600 ml/1 pint water
300–450 ml/½–¾ pint dry white wine
salt
2 tomatoes, peeled, seeded and diced

GARNISH
thin lemon wedges

1. Ask your fishmonger to clean mackerel and remove heads (to keep for the *court-bouillon*).

2. Make a *court-bouillon* with heads of fish, sliced lemon, carrots, diced onion and green pepper, thyme, bay leaves, peppercorns, cloves, water and dry white wine. Salt generously and cook for 30 minutes. Add diced tomatoes.

3. Place fish in a flat flameproof dish. Pour hot *court-bouillon* over them and cook fish in *court-bouillon* for about 15 minutes, or until they flake easily with a fork. Allow fish to cool in their liquor with aromatics.

4. Just before serving, garnish with thin lemon wedges.

Whitebait Fried in Lard

675 g/1½ lb whitebait
ice cubes and iced water
seasoned flour
lard for deep-frying
salt and freshly ground black pepper
lemon wedges

1. Put whitebait in a shallow bowl with ice cubes and a little iced water. Leave for 10 minutes.

77

2. Just before frying, spread fish on a clean tea towel to dry. Place on paper liberally dusted with well-seasoned flour and dredge with more flour. Place in a wire basket and shake off surplus flour. Then plunge the basket into very hot lard and fry quickly for 3 to 5 minutes, shaking basket continually to keep fish apart while cooking.

3. Lift basket from fat and shake it well before transferring fish to kitchen paper to drain. Place whitebait on a heated serving dish in a warm oven and repeat until all the whitebait are fried. Season with salt and freshly ground black pepper, and serve with lemon wedges.

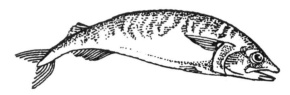

New England Fish Balls

350 g/12 oz salt cod
2 level tablespoons grated onion
4 tablespoons milk or cream
freshly ground black pepper
350 g/12 oz cooked potatoes, mashed
2 eggs
flour
butter or olive oil
French Tomato Sauce (see page 83)

1. Soak cod overnight in a bowl under gently running water. Drain and place in a saucepan. Cover with cold water and bring slowly to the boil. Drain and return to saucepan. Cover with cold water and bring to the boil again. Remove from heat and allow to steep in hot water for 10 minutes. Drain and flake, removing skin and bones.

2. Combine grated onion, milk, (or cream), freshly ground black pepper, cod and mashed potatoes. Bind with raw egg. If mixture is too dry, add a little more milk.

3. Shape mixture into small balls, flour them and brown on both sides in a little hot butter or oil, or a combination of the two. Serve with Tomato Sauce.

Mousseline de Brochet Homardine

78

1 small lobster (about 350 g/12 oz)
olive oil
2 shallots, finely chopped
300 ml/½ pint dry white wine
150 ml/¼ pint Madeira
salt and freshly ground black pepper
2 level tablespoons flour
10 tablespoons butter
450 ml/¾ pint double cream
350 g/12 oz fresh pike (after skin and bones
  have been removed)
450 g/1 lb spinach
4 tablespoons chicken stock
4 large mushrooms
fresh breadcrumbs
crescents of flaky pastry (optional)

1. Cut lobster tail (shell and all) into slices; cut remaining body in half lengthwise and remove the coral. Carefully remove the intestinal tube. Sauté lobster pieces in olive oil over a high heat for 3 minutes. Add finely chopped shallots and moisten with dry white wine and Madeira. Season to taste with salt and freshly ground black pepper, and cook for 15 minutes. Remove lobster pieces from pan.

2. Add flour and 2 tablespoons butter to lobster coral. Mix well and add to pan juices, stirring until sauce is well blended. Pour sauce into the top of a double saucepan, add 150 ml/¼ pint double cream and allow to simmer over water until ready to serve.

3. To make mousseline: mince pike through the finest blade of your mincer. Place minced pike in a mortar, season to taste with salt and freshly ground black pepper, and pound it to a smooth paste, adding remaining double cream gradually to create a smooth, firm mousse. Oil 4 pieces of waxed paper. Divide pike mousse into 5 equal parts and put 1 portion of the mixture on each of 4 pieces of paper together with a *medaillon* of lobster tail (with shell removed). Fold each packet into a 'finger' 10 cm/4 inches long and 5 cm/2 inches thick. Poach them in simmering salted water for 15 minutes.

4. To make spinach mousses: wash spinach carefully, drain and cook with 4 tablespoons each butter and chicken stock. Drain until fairly dry. Put through the mincer with remaining pike *mousseline.* Season with salt and freshly ground black pepper, and mix well. Butter 4 individual aspic moulds and line with spinach mixture, placing remaining lobster meat, finely chopped, in the centre. Cover with the remaining spinach and poach in a *bain-marie* for 20 minutes.

5. To stuff mushroom caps: wash mushroom caps. Finely chop the stalks. Mix chopped stalks with 4 tablespoons softened butter, and stuff mushroom caps with this mixture. Sprinkle with freshly grated breadcrumbs and bake in a moderately hot oven (190°C, 375°F, Gas Mark 5) on a buttered baking sheet.

6. To serve: unfold the *mousselines* of pike. Arrange them in the centre of a long serving dish, mask with half the sauce (putting the rest in a sauceboat) and keep warm.

7. Remove lobster-filled spinach mousses carefully from the moulds and garnish the dish with them together with the mushroom caps. Add flaky pastry crescents if desired.

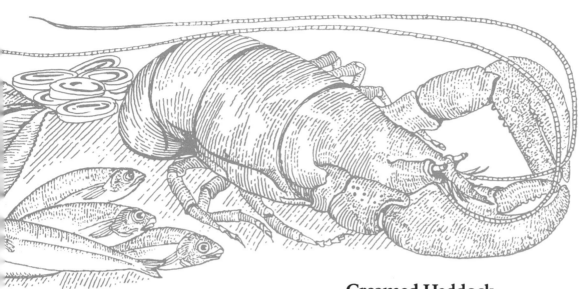

Sardines Farcies aux Épinards

1.5 kg/3 lb fresh spinach
olive oil
2 cloves garlic
1 Spanish onion, finely chopped
salt and freshly ground black pepper
18 fresh sardines (heads, tails and backbones
   removed)
fresh breadcrumbs

1. Wash spinach carefully and remove stems. Drain well and cook until limp. Place in a saucepan with 2 tablespoons olive oil, stirring constantly. Drain spinach and then chop finely with garlic.

2. Sauté finely chopped onion in 4 tablespoons olive oil until golden. Add finely chopped spinach and season to taste with salt and freshly ground black pepper. Mix well. Spread two-thirds of spinach mixture in the bottom of a *gratin* dish.

3. Place prepared sardines open side up on a clean tea towel. Place a tablespoon of reserved spinach mixture on each sardine half. Roll fish up tightly (starting at the head) and place them in rows on the bed of spinach. Sprinkle with breadcrumbs and then with olive oil, and bake in a moderate oven (190°C, 375°F, Gas Mark 5) for 20 minutes, or until done.

Creamed Haddock

Illustrated on page 88

1 kg/2 lb smoked haddock
milk
water
3 level tablespoons butter
3 level tablespoons flour
450 ml/¾ pint double cream
freshly ground black pepper
freshly grated nutmeg
100 g/4 oz small Norwegian prawns,
   defrosted
triangles of bread sautéed in butter

1. Cook haddock in equal quantities of milk and water until just tender. Allow to cool in stock. Drain, reserving stock, and remove bits of skin and bones from fish.

2. Melt butter in the top of a double saucepan. Stir in flour and cook over water for 3 minutes, stirring continuously until smooth. Add cream and stock the fish was cooked in, and continue to cook, stirring from time to time. Season to taste with freshly ground black pepper and a little grated nutmeg.

3. Fold prawns and haddock pieces (with skin and bones removed) into sauce and simmer gently until heated through. Serve in a shallow casserole, surrounded by triangles of bread sautéed in butter.

80

Anchovy Salad

225–350 g/8–12 oz salted anchovies
1 medium-sized onion, finely chopped
4 level tablespoons finely chopped parsley
4 thin slices lemon
4 tablespoons olive oil
4 tablespoons red wine
freshly ground black pepper

1. Wash anchovies in water until liquid is clear; dry them with a clean cloth and remove heads, tails and fins. Strip anchovy fillets from bones and place in a bowl. Add finely chopped onion, parsley and lemon slices.

2. Combine olive oil and red wine and pour over fillets. Season to taste with freshly ground black pepper and marinate anchovies for at least 2 hours before serving.

Filets de Sole au Vermouth

2 fillets of sole (about 675 g/1½ lb each)
melted butter
2 level tablespoons finely chopped onion
6 tablespoons dry vermouth
1 level tablespoon tomato purée
salt and freshly ground black pepper
150 ml/¼ pint double cream
1 truffle, or parsley, finely chopped
crescents of flaky pastry (see page 91)

1. Place fillets of sole in a well-buttered flameproof *gratin* dish. Scatter with finely chopped onion.

2. Blend vermouth, 6 tablespoons melted butter and tomato purée and pour over fish. Season to taste with salt and freshly ground black pepper. Cook over a high heat until fish flakes easily with a fork. Add double cream and simmer gently for a minute or two, shaking the pan continuously so that the sauce will thicken gradually.

3. To serve: place fish fillets on a heated serving dish. Pour over sauce, sprinkle with finely chopped truffle or parsley, and garnish with several crescents of flaky pastry. Serve immediately.

Rougets en Papillote 'Baumanière'

4 small rougets (red mullet),
  100–150 g/4–5 oz each
olive oil
salt and freshly ground black pepper
4 bay leaves
4 thin rashers bacon, grilled
fat or olive oil for deep-frying
4 slices lemon
4 anchovy fillets

SAUCE
4–5 egg whites
300 ml/½ pint double cream
4–5 anchovy fillets, mashed
salt and freshly ground black pepper
freshly grated nutmeg

1. *Rougets* are not gutted before cooking. Just sprinkle each fish with olive oil and season to taste with salt and freshly ground black pepper. Place 1 bay leaf on one side of fish and a thin rasher of grilled bacon on the other side.

2. Cut 4 pieces of greaseproof paper approximately 21 by 28 cm/8½ by 11 inches. Fold in half and cut in heart shapes. Open, brush with oil, and place prepared fish, bay leaf and bacon on one half. Fold paper shape over and seal edges well by crimping them together. Sauté *papillotes* in deep fat or olive oil for about 18 minutes.

3. Arrange *papillotes* on a serving dish. Open each one carefully and decorate *rougets* with lemon and anchovy. Serve with the following sauce.

4. To make sauce: beat egg whites until stiff and whip cream. Combine the two, add mashed anchovy fillets, and season to taste with salt, freshly ground black pepper and grated nutmeg. Cook over boiling water, skimming constantly, until heated through. Strain and serve hot.

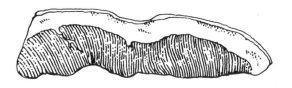

Brochettes of Cod and Sole with Mustard Sauce *Serves 4*
Grilled Herrings
Bouillabaisse de Morue *Serves 6 to 8*

Brochettes of Cod and Sole with Mustard Sauce

2 thick cod steaks
2 small fillets of sole
salt
flour
oil for frying

MUSTARD SAUCE
2 level tablespoons butter
1 tablespoon olive oil
1 onion, coarsely chopped
1 bunch parsley stalks
salt and freshly ground black pepper
2 level tablespoons flour
300 ml/½ pint canned clam juice
150 ml/¼ pint dry white wine
1–2 level tablespoons Dijon mustard

1. To make mustard sauce: heat butter and oil in a saucepan. Add chopped onion and parsley stalks, season to taste with salt and freshly ground black pepper, and sauté, stirring continuously, until onion is transparent. Sprinkle with flour and stir until well blended. Add clam juice and wine, and simmer gently for 20 minutes. Place mustard in the top of a double saucepan and strain stock over it, pressing onion and parsley stalks well against sieve with a wooden spoon. Mix well over water and continue to cook until sauce is thick and smooth.

2. When ready to serve: cut fish into 2.5-cm/ 1-inch squares and arrange them on small skewers. Salt and flour them, and deep-fry in very hot oil until golden. Serve *brochettes* immediately, accompanied by sauce.

Grilled Herrings

1. Clean and scale fresh herrings, taking care not to break the delicate skin underneath. Cut off heads. Wash and dry herrings carefully.

2. Make 2 shallow incisions on sides of each fish with a sharp knife.

3. Dip herrings in seasoned flour and then in melted butter. Sprinkle with lemon juice and grill on a well-oiled baking sheet for 5 to 8 minutes on each side, until they are cooked through. Serve immediately with lemon wedges or with Hollandaise Sauce (see Fresh Asparagus Hollandaise, page 16) or Mustard Hollandaise.

Bouillabaisse de Morue

675 g/1½ lb salt cod
2 Spanish onions, sliced
2 leeks (white parts only), sliced
4 tablespoons olive oil
4 tomatoes, peeled, seeded and diced
2 level tablespoons butter
1.15 litres/2 pints water
1 bouquet garni (2 sprigs thyme, 1 sprig fennel, 1 bay leaf)
1 strip orange peel
2 cloves garlic, crushed
¼ level teaspoon powdered saffron
freshly ground black pepper
1 kg/2 lb potatoes, peeled and sliced
French bread
garlic
grated cheese
finely chopped parsley

1. Soak salt cod overnight. Drain and cut into large cubes.

2. Sauté sliced onions and leeks in olive oil until transparent. Simmer tomatoes in butter until smooth. Fill a large saucepan with water. Add vegetables with *bouquet garni*, orange peel, crushed garlic and saffron, and season to taste with freshly ground black pepper. Bring to the boil, add sliced potatoes, and when they are half cooked, add cubed salt cod. Lower heat and simmer *bouillabaisse* until cod is tender.

3. To serve: place slices of stale French bread rubbed with garlic and sprinkled with grated cheese in individual soup dishes. Pour over *bouillon*. Serve cod and potatoes on a separate serving dish, sprinkled with finely chopped parsley.

81

Steamed Salt Cod in the Italian Manner *Serves 4 to 6*
Poached Fillet of Sole with Grapes *Serves 4*
Baked Herrings

82

Steamed Salt Cod in the Italian Manner

1 kg/2 lb salt cod

SAUCE
**4 level tablespoons finely chopped Spanish
   onion
6 level tablespoons finely chopped parsley
2 cloves garlic, finely chopped
8 tablespoons olive oil
juice of ½ large lemon
pinch of monosodium glutamate
salt and freshly ground black pepper**

1. Soak cod overnight in a bowl under gently running water. Drain and put salt cod in a saucepan. Cover with cold water and bring to the boil. Drain and return to saucepan. Cover with cold water and bring to the boil again. Turn off heat and allow to steep in hot water for 10 minutes. Drain and remove skin and bones.

2. Combine first 5 sauce ingredients; add monosodium glutamate, and salt and freshly ground black pepper, to taste. Chill. When ready to serve, pour sauce over poached (or steamed) salt cod.

Poached Fillet of Sole with Grapes

**3 tablespoons softened butter
3 shallots or 1 small onion, finely chopped
8 fillets of sole
salt and freshly ground black pepper
150 ml/¼ pint dry white wine
150 ml/¼ pint fish stock (made with fish
   trimmings and ½ chicken stock cube)
150 ml/¼ pint thick Cream Sauce (see
   Omelette Bénédictine, page 24)
1 egg yolk
175 g/6 oz seedless white grapes
4-8 level tablespoons whipped cream**

1. Spread 2 tablespoons butter in a shallow pan and sprinkle with finely chopped shallots or onion. Season fillets of sole to taste with salt and freshly

ground black pepper. Roll them up, fasten with wooden cocktail sticks and arrange in the pan. Moisten with dry white wine and fish stock. Cover fish with a circle of buttered greaseproof paper cut the size of the pan, with a small hole in the middle. Bring to the boil, cover the pan and poach gently for 10 to 12 minutes. Remove wooden sticks from fillets and arrange fish on a heated dish.

2. Cook the fish liquor until it is reduced to about a quarter of the original quantity. Strain, add Cream Sauce mixed with egg yolk, and warm through until smooth. Do not allow to boil.

3. Simmer small seedless white grapes in a little water for a few minutes. Drain, simmer in 1 tablespoon butter and pour around fish.

4. Fold whipped cream into the sauce. Pour it over the fish and brown under a hot grill until golden.

Baked Herrings

1. Clean and scale fresh herrings, taking care not to break the delicate skin underneath. Cut off heads. Wash and dry herrings carefully.

2. Remove roes, detach skin and pound roes with an equal amount of softened butter. Force mixture through a fine sieve. Mix in 2 to 4 tablespoons fresh breadcrumbs, flavour with finely chopped parsley, and season to taste with salt and freshly ground black pepper.

3. Slit herrings down backbone with a sharp knife and remove backbone carefully, snipping both ends free with kitchen scissors.

4. Stuff herrings with roe mixture and place fish in a lightly-buttered shallow ovenproof dish. Sprinkle lightly with breadcrumbs, finely chopped parsley and melted butter.

5. Cover fish with buttered paper and bake in a moderately hot oven (200°C, 400°F, Gas Mark 6) for 15 to 20 minutes, until cooked through. Just before serving, brown under grill. Serve with lemon wedges.

Sauces

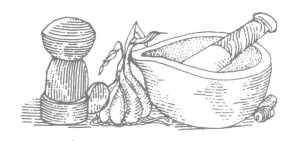

Basic Brown Sauce

2 tablespoons butter
I small onion, thinly sliced
2 tablespoons flour
750 ml/I¼ pints well-flavoured brown stock
I small carrot
I small turnip
I stick celery or ¼ teaspoon celery seed
4 mushrooms
2-4 tomatoes or I-2 tablespoons tomato
   purée
I bouquet garni (3 sprigs parsley, I sprig
   thyme, I bay leaf)
2 cloves
I2 black peppercorns
salt

I. Heat butter in a thick-bottomed saucepan until it browns. Add thinly sliced onion and simmer, stirring constantly, until golden. Stir in flour and cook, stirring constantly, for a minute or two longer.

2. The good colour of your sauce depends upon the thorough browning of these ingredients without allowing them to burn. When this is accomplished, remove saucepan from the heat and pour in the stock. Return to heat and stir until it comes to the boil. Allow to boil for 5 minutes, skimming all scum from the top with a perforated spoon.

3. Wash and slice carrot, turnip, celery, mushrooms and tomatoes, and add them with the *bouquet garni*, cloves, peppercorns, and salt, to taste. Simmer the sauce gently for at least 30 minutes stirring occasionally and skimming when necessary. Strain through a fine sieve. Remove fat and reheat before serving.

Vinaigrette Sauce

I tablespoon lemon juice
I-2 tablespoons wine vinegar
¼-½ level teaspoon dry mustard
coarse salt and freshly ground black pepper
6-8 tablespoons olive oil

I. Mix together lemon juice, wine vinegar and dry mustard, and season to taste with coarse salt and freshly ground black pepper.

2. Add olive oil, and beat with a fork until the mixture emulsifies.

French Tomato Sauce

2 tablespoons butter
2 tablespoons finely chopped ham
I small carrot, finely chopped
I small turnip, finely chopped
I onion, finely chopped
I stick celery, finely chopped
6-8 ripe tomatoes, sliced
2 tablespoons tomato purée
I tablespoon flour
I bouquet garni (I sprig each thyme,
   marjoram and parsley)
300 ml/½ pint well-flavoured beef stock
salt and freshly ground black pepper
lemon juice
sugar

I. Melt butter in a thick-bottomed saucepan. Add finely chopped ham and vegetables, and sauté mixture until onion is transparent and soft.

2. Stir in sliced tomatoes and tomato purée. Simmer for a minute or two, sprinkle with flour and mix well. Then add *bouquet garni* and beef stock and simmer gently, stirring continuously, until sauce comes to the boil. Season to taste with salt and freshly ground black pepper and simmer gently for 30 minutes, stirring from time to time. If the sauce becomes too thick, add a little more stock.

3. Strain sauce through a fine sieve. Reheat and add lemon juice and sugar, to taste.

Béchamel Sauce

84

3 tablespoons butter
½ onion, minced
2 tablespoons flour
600 ml/1 pint hot milk
2 tablespoons lean veal or ham, chopped
1 small sprig thyme
½ bay leaf
white peppercorns
freshly grated nutmeg

1. In a thick-bottomed saucepan, or in the top of a double saucepan, melt 2 tablespoons butter and cook onion in it over a low heat until transparent. Stir in flour and cook for a few minutes, stirring constantly, until mixture cooks through but does not take on colour.

2. Add hot milk and cook, stirring constantly, until the mixture is thick and smooth.

3. In another saucepan, simmer finely chopped lean veal or ham in 1 tablespoon butter over a very low heat. Season with thyme, bay leaf, white peppercorns and grated nutmeg. Cook for 5 minutes, stirring to keep veal from browning.

4. Add veal to the sauce and cook over hot water for 45 minutes to 1 hour, stirring occasionally. When reduced to the proper consistency (two-thirds of the original quantity), strain sauce through a fine sieve into a bowl, pressing meat and onion well to extract all the liquid. Cover surface of sauce with tiny pieces of butter to keep film from forming.

For a richer Béchamel, remove the saucepan from the heat, add 1 or 2 egg yolks, and heat through. Do not let sauce come to the boil after adding eggs or it will curdle.

Basic Meat Aspic

225 g/8 oz beef bones
duck or chicken carcass, if available
1 calf's foot or 4 cleaned chicken feet
1 Spanish onion, sliced
1 large leek, sliced
2 large carrots, sliced
2 sticks celery, chopped
1.15 litres/2 pints water
salt and freshly ground black pepper
1 bouquet garni (parsley, 1 sprig thyme, 1 bay leaf)
1 egg white
100 g/4 oz raw lean beef, chopped
1 teaspoon finely chopped chervil and tarragon

1. Combine first ten ingredients in a large stock-pot. Bring slowly to the boil and simmer gently for about 4 hours, removing scum from time to time. Strain and cool before skimming off the fat.

2. **To clarify the stock:** beat egg white lightly, and combine with chopped raw lean beef and chopped herbs in the bottom of a large saucepan. Add the cooled stock and mix well. Bring stock slowly to the boil, stirring constantly. Lower the heat and simmer the stock very gently for about 15 minutes. Strain through a flannel cloth while still hot. Allow stock to cool and then stir in one of the following:

SHERRY ASPIC
Stir in 4 tablespoons dry sherry

MADEIRA ASPIC
Stir in 4 tablespoons Madeira

PORT ASPIC
Stir in 4 tablespoons port wine

TARRAGON ASPIC
When clarifying aspic, add 6 additional sprigs of tarragon

Note: This recipe will make 1.15 litres/2 pints of jelly and will keep for several days in the refrigerator.

Chilled Spanish Soup (see page 73)

Chilled Asparagus Soup (see page 75)
Maquereaux en Court-Bouillon (see page 77)

Brandade de Morue (Cream of Salt Cod) (see page 76)

Creamed Haddock (see page 79)

Mayonnaise

89

2 egg yolks
salt and freshly ground black pepper
½ teaspoon Dijon mustard
lemon juice
300 ml/½ pint olive oil

1. Place egg yolks (make sure gelatinous thread of the egg is removed), salt, freshly ground black pepper and mustard in a bowl. Twist a cloth wrung out in very cold water round the bottom of the bowl to keep it steady and cool. Using a wire whisk, fork or wooden spoon, beat the yolks to a smooth paste.

2. Add a few drops of lemon juice (the acid helps the emulsion), and beat in about a quarter of the oil, drop by drop. Add a little more lemon juice to the mixture and then, a little more quickly now, add more oil, beating all the while. Continue adding oil and beating until the sauce is of a good thick consistency. Correct seasoning (more salt, freshly ground black pepper and lemon juice) as desired. If you are making the mayonnaise a day before using it, stir in 1 tablespoon boiling water when it is of the desired consistency. This will keep it from turning or separating.

Note: If the mayonnaise should curdle, break another egg yolk into a clean bowl and gradually beat the curdled mayonnaise into it. Your mayonnaise will begin to 'take' immediately.

If mayonnaise is to be used for a salad, thin it down considerably with dry white wine, vinegar or lemon juice. If it is to be used for coating meat, poultry or fish, add a little liquid aspic to stiffen it.

If sauce is to be kept for several hours before serving, cover the bowl with a cloth wrung out in very cold water to prevent a skin from forming on the top.

Aïoli Sauce

4 fat cloves of garlic per person
1 egg yolk for each 2 persons
salt
olive oil
freshly ground black pepper
lemon juice

1. Take 4 fat cloves of garlic per person and 1 egg yolk for each 2 persons. Crush garlic to a smooth paste in a mortar with a little salt; blend in egg yolks until mixture is a smooth, homogeneous mass.

2. Now add olive oil, drop by drop at first, a thin, fine trickle later, whisking the mixture as you would for a mayonnaise. The *aïoli* will thicken gradually until it reaches a stiff, firm consistency. The exact quantity of oil is, of course, determined by the number of egg yolks used.

3. Season to taste with additional salt, a little pepper and lemon juice. This sauce is served chilled, in a bowl. Guests help themselves.

Aïoli Sauce Without Eggs

4-6 cloves garlic
1 boiled potato, chilled
lemon juice
salt and freshly ground black pepper
olive oil

1. Peel garlic and boiled potato.

2. Pound garlic in a mortar until smooth; add potato and pound until it is well mixed with garlic. Add a little lemon juice, salt and freshly ground black pepper, to taste.

3. Then, drop by drop, whisk in olive oil as you would for mayonnaise, until *aïoli* is thick and smooth. Correct seasoning and serve.

90

Shortcrust Pastry for Savoury Tarts and Pies

225 g/8 oz plain flour
1 teaspoon castor sugar
squeeze of lemon juice
pinch of salt
100 g/4 oz butter, diced
1-3 tablespoons iced water

1. Sift flour and sugar into a mixing bowl. Add lemon juice, salt and butter. Cover well with the flour and rub together lightly with the tips of the fingers until the mixture resembles fine breadcrumbs. While rubbing, keep lifting the flour well up in the bowl, so that air may mix with it and the butter is not made too soft.

2. When pastry is thoroughly mixed, make a well in the centre and add cold water very gradually, mixing with one hand or a knife. Add very little water or pastry will be tough instead of short.

3. Sprinkle the pastry board with flour. Lay the dough on it and work lightly with the hands until free from cracks. Flour a rolling pin. Press down the pastry and then with sharp quick strokes roll pastry on one side only to the thickness required. Roll pastry lightly and try to press equally with both hands. Never allow pastry to stick on the board, but lift occasionally on the rolling pin and dust some flour underneath. If anything has stuck to the board, scrape it off carefully with a knife before beginning to roll again. Always sprinkle flour over board and pastry through a flour sifter to make it finer and lighter, using as little flour as possible for this, as too much tends to make the pastry hard. If the rolling pin sticks to the pastry, dust with a little flour and brush it off again lightly with a small brush kept for this purpose.

4. To bake pastry: a fairly hot oven is required for pastry, for if it is not hot enough the butter will melt and run out before the starch grains in the flour have had time to burst and absorb it. If the oven is too hot, however, the pastry will burn before it has risen properly. When baking pastry, open and close the door as gently as possible and never more often than is absolutely necessary. If pastry becomes too brown before it has cooked sufficiently, cover it over with a piece of aluminium foil or a double sheet of paper that has been lightly sprinkled with water. If the pastry is not to be used at once when taken from the oven, allow it to cool slowly in the warm kitchen. Light pastry becomes heavy if cooled too quickly.

TO BAKE 'BLIND'
Line a pie tin with pastry, fluting the edges. Chill. Prick bottom with a fork and cover bottom of pastry with a piece of waxed paper or aluminium foil. Cover with dried beans and bake in a hot oven (230°C, 450°F, Gas Mark 8) for about 15 minutes, just long enough to set the crust without browning it. Remove beans and paper or foil and allow to cool. Fill with desired filling and bake in a moderately hot oven (190°C, 375°F, Gas Mark 5) until done. The beans can be reserved in a storage jar and used again.

TO BAKE PASTRY CASE ONLY
Bake 'blind' as above for 15 minutes. Remove beans and foil, lower heat to 190°C, 375°F, Gas Mark 5 and bake for 10 to 15 minutes. If crust becomes too brown at edges, cover rim with a little crumpled foil.

RICH BISCUIT CRUST
A richer pastry can be made in the same way, using 150-175 g/5-6 oz butter and adding the yolk of 1 egg beaten with a little water for mixing.

Puff Pastry (Pâte Feuilletée)

225 g/8 oz plain flour
generous pinch of salt
squeeze of lemon juice
225 g/8 oz butter, finely diced
1-3 tablespoons iced water

1. Sift flour and salt into a clean, dry mixing bowl, and add lemon juice and a quarter of the diced butter. Rub together lightly with the tips of your fingers until the mixture resembles fine breadcrumbs. Then mix with just enough iced water to make a rather stiff dough. Turn this out on to a floured board and work it well with the hands until it no longer sticks to the fingers and is perfectly smooth.

2. Roll it rather thinly into a square or round shape.

3. The remaining butter to be used should be as nearly as possible of the same consistency as the dough, so work it with your hands into a neat thin cake and place it in the centre of the dough. Fold dough up rather loosely, and flatten the folds with a rolling pin. Then roll the pastry out into a long, narrow strip, being careful not to allow the butter to break through.

4. Fold dough exactly in three. Press down the folds and lay the pastry aside in a cool place for at least 15 minutes. This is called giving the pastry one 'turn'; seven of these operations are usually required for puff pastry.

5. The next time the pastry is rolled, place it with the joins at your right-hand side and the open end towards you. Give it two turns this time, and again put it in the refrigerator for at least 15 minutes. Repeat this until the pastry has had seven rolls in all, one roll or turn the first time, and after that two each time with an interval between. The object of cooling the pastry between rolls is to keep the butter and flour in the distinct and separate layers (in which the rolling and folding has arranged them), and on which the lightness of your pastry depends. When rolling, keep the pressure of your hands on the rolling pin as even as possible.

6. After you have given the pastry its last roll, put it in the refrigerator for 30 minutes before using it, then roll to the required thickness.

Note: This pastry will keep for several days in the refrigerator if wrapped in a piece of waxed paper or in a damp cloth.

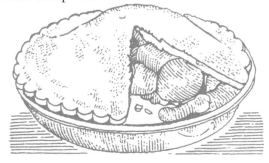

Flaky Pastry

275 g/10 oz plain flour
generous pinch of salt
squeeze of lemon juice
200 g/7 oz butter
1–3 tablespoons iced water

1. Sift the flour and salt into a clean, dry bowl and add lemon juice.

2. Divide butter into 4 equal parts. Take one of these pieces and rub it into the flour with the tips of the fingers until mixture is quite free from lumps. Then add just enough iced water to form dough into one lump. Mix with hands as lightly as possible and turn out on to a floured board. Knead lightly until free from cracks, and then roll out into a long narrow strip, rather less than 5 mm/$\frac{1}{4}$ inch in thickness.

3. Take one of the remaining portions of butter, and with the point of a knife put it in even rows of small pieces all over the pastry, leaving a 2.5-cm/1-inch margin without butter round the edges. (If butter is too hard, work it on a plate with a knife before commencing.)

4. Now flour the surface lightly and fold the pastry exactly in three. Turn the pastry half round, bringing the joins to the right-hand side, and press the folds down sharply with the rolling pin so as to enclose some air.

5. Roll the pastry out again into a long narrow strip, and proceed as before until the two remaining portions of butter have been used. If the butter becomes too soft during the rolling, refrigerate the pastry for a short time before completing the process.

6. The last time, roll the pastry out to the desired thickness, and if it requires widening, turn it across the board and roll across. Never roll in a slanting direction, or the lightness of the pastry will suffer.

Note: This pastry is not quite as rich as puff pastry. It may be kept for several days in the refrigerator if wrapped in waxed paper or in a damp cloth.

Index